The Psychology of Growing Minds:

How Age Reshapes Thought and Emotion

How Age Reshapes Thought and Emotion

The Psychology of Growing Minds

Published By: Wissira Research Lab LLC

Imprint Name: Wissira Press

US Office: Carmel, United States- 46074

India Office: KDP, RNE, India-201017

Email: editor@wissira.us, **Website:** https://books.wissira.us

Mobile: +91 7535 916 555

Prof. Dr. Anu Kant Mital

Kishore Raipurkar

Dhanashri Rajshri Ravindra Jadhav

Krithika Tharan

ISBN - 978-93-7559-730-8

Maharaja Agrasen Himalayan Garhwal University,

Address: Uttarakhand, India

Edition: 2026

Printed In: India

How Age Reshapes Thought and Emotion

Maharaja Agrasen Himalayan Garhwal University,

Address: Uttarakhand, India

The Psychology of Growing Minds:

How Age Reshapes Thought and Emotion

2026

Authors:

Prof. Dr. Anu Kant Mital

Kishore Raipurkar

Dhanashri Rajshri Ravindra Jadhav

Krithika Tharan

Published By

Wissira Research Lab

ISBN 978-93-75597-30-8

9 789375 597308

Preface

Human development is often viewed as a sequence of milestones-childhood, adolescence, adulthood, and old age-each treated as a separate psychological chapter. Yet the human mind does not grow in isolated segments. Thought, emotion, and behaviour evolve continuously, shaped by age, experience, relationships, and the broader social world. *The Psychology of Growing Minds: How Age Reshapes Thought and Emotion* is written with the conviction that understanding this lifelong journey is essential not only for students of psychology but for educators, caregivers, policymakers, and individuals seeking deeper insight into themselves and others.

This book adopts a **lifespan perspective**, emphasizing that psychological growth does not end with childhood or adolescence. Instead, each stage of life introduces new ways of thinking, feeling, and relating to the world. From the sensory foundations of infancy to the reflective wisdom of late adulthood, development is presented as a dynamic process involving both continuity and change. By tracing this progression, the book highlights how early experiences influence later functioning, while also recognizing the capacity for growth, adaptation, and resilience at every age.

A central aim of this work is to integrate **cognitive and emotional development** within their social and cultural contexts. Too often, psychological texts isolate thinking from feeling, or individual development from social influence. This book brings these elements together, showing how cognition, emotion, identity, and relationships interact across the lifespan. The discussion draws upon established psychological theories while remaining accessible, making complex ideas understandable without oversimplification.

The chapters are organized to reflect key developmental periods, each explored through thematic sections that examine reasoning, emotional regulation, identity formation, and social roles. Practical illustrations and case examples are used to connect theory with lived experience, reinforcing the relevance of developmental psychology to everyday life. Throughout the book, emphasis is placed on psychological well-being, ethical understanding, and the importance of supportive environments in fostering healthy development.

This book is intended for undergraduate and postgraduate students of psychology, education, and social sciences, as well as for professionals working with individuals across age groups. It may also serve as a reflective guide for readers interested in understanding their own developmental journeys. By presenting development as a shared human process, the book encourages empathy, self-awareness, and respect for the evolving nature of the human mind.

Ultimately, *The Psychology of Growing Minds* seeks to remind readers that growth is not defined by age alone, but by the ongoing interaction between mind, emotion, and experience. Recognizing this interconnected journey allows us to better support learning, mental health, and human flourishing across the entire lifespan.

Authors:

Prof. Dr. Anu Kant Mital

Kishore Raipurkar

Dhanashri Rajshri Ravindra Jadhav

Krithika Tharan

Overview of the Book

The Psychology of Growing Minds: How Age Reshapes Thought and Emotion offers a comprehensive exploration of human psychological development from infancy to late adulthood. The book is grounded in the lifespan perspective, presenting development as a continuous and evolving process rather than a set of disconnected stages. It examines how cognitive abilities, emotional responses, identity, and social relationships transform with age, shaped by biological maturation, personal experience, and cultural context.

The book begins by establishing foundational concepts in developmental psychology, emphasizing the interaction between biological, psychological, and environmental factors. Early chapters focus on infancy and early childhood, highlighting how perception, attachment, language, imagination, and emotional expression form the building blocks of later development. These chapters underscore the significance of early experiences in shaping emotional security, learning capacity, and social behaviour.

As the narrative progresses, the book examines middle childhood and adolescence, stages marked by expanding reasoning abilities, moral understanding, identity exploration, and heightened emotional sensitivity. These chapters address the growing influence of peers, education, and social expectations, explaining how individuals learn to regulate emotions, evaluate values, and make increasingly complex decisions. Special attention is given to the challenges and opportunities of adolescence, a period of rapid psychological change and self-definition.

The later chapters shift focus to adulthood and aging, exploring how cognitive maturity, emotional intelligence, and life experience contribute to psychological stability and meaning. Early and middle adulthood are discussed in terms of intimacy, responsibility, generativity, and role transitions, while late adulthood highlights wisdom, emotional resilience, and adaptation to change. Rather than viewing aging as decline, the book emphasizes growth, reflection, and the continued potential for psychological well-being.

Throughout the book, theory is integrated with real-life illustrations to connect academic concepts with everyday experiences. The concluding chapter synthesizes insights across all life stages, reinforcing the idea that development involves both continuity and transformation. By adopting a holistic and inclusive approach, the book encourages readers to appreciate the complexity of human growth and to recognize the enduring capacity for learning, emotional balance, and self-understanding across the lifespan.

Overall, this book serves as both an academic resource and a reflective guide, offering readers a structured yet accessible understanding of how age reshapes thought and emotion, and how psychological development remains an ongoing journey throughout life.

Table of Contents

1

Understanding Human Development Across the Lifespan

1.1 Development as a Lifelong Psychological Process

Human development is not confined to childhood or adolescence; it is a continuous process that unfolds from birth to old age. Psychological growth involves gradual changes in thinking, emotional responses, behaviour, and self-understanding.

Development as a Lifelong Psychological Process refers to the understanding that human psychological growth does not stop at a particular age but continues throughout the entire lifespan. Rather than being limited to early childhood or teenage years, development unfolds gradually from infancy through adulthood and into old age, shaped by biological maturation, social relationships, cultural context, and personal experiences.

At each stage of life, individuals experience changes in **cognition**, **emotion**, **behaviour**, and **self-concept**. Early experiences lay important foundations-for example, attachment patterns formed in childhood can influence later relationships-but these foundations are not rigid or irreversible. New environments, roles, responsibilities, and challenges constantly interact with earlier learning, allowing people to revise beliefs, acquire new skills, and adapt emotionally. This explains why adults can still learn, change careers, reshape values, or develop new coping strategies later in life.

Viewing development as lifelong highlights the **dynamic and adaptive nature of the human mind**. Psychological characteristics such as personality traits, emotional regulation, and moral reasoning are not permanently fixed; instead, they show degrees of continuity and change. Life transitions-such as entering the workforce, becoming a parent, experiencing loss, or aging-often prompt reflection and psychological growth, encouraging individuals to adjust their perspectives and behaviours.

This perspective also emphasizes resilience and potential. Even in later adulthood, people continue to develop through reflection, wisdom, and emotional refinement. Understanding development as a continuous process helps explain individual differences across ages and underscores that growth, learning, and transformation are possible at every stage of life, making human psychology a lifelong journey rather than a time-bound phase.

1.2 Interaction of Biology, Environment, and Experience

Psychological development emerges from the interaction between biological maturation and environmental influences. Genetic factors shape brain growth and temperament, while family, culture, education, and social relationships guide how these biological capacities are expressed.

Interaction of Biology, Environment, and Experience highlights that psychological development is not driven by a single force but by the continuous interplay of multiple influences. Biological factors such as genetics, brain maturation, and hormonal changes provide the basic framework for development. These biological foundations influence traits like temperament, energy levels, emotional sensitivity, and learning potential. However, biology alone does not determine how an individual thinks, feels, or behaves across life.

Environmental influences shape how biological potentials are expressed. Family structure, parenting styles, cultural norms, educational systems, peer groups, and socioeconomic conditions all play a crucial role in guiding development. For example, a child may be biologically predisposed to strong cognitive abilities, but access to quality education and stimulation determines how fully those abilities develop. Similarly, cultural values influence emotional expression, social behaviour, and moral reasoning, shaping psychological outcomes beyond genetic predispositions.

Personal experiences act as powerful modifiers within this interaction. Experiences such as nurturing or neglectful caregiving, exposure to stress or trauma, opportunities for learning, and availability of social support significantly affect emotional regulation, critical thinking skills, and self-concept. Positive experiences can strengthen resilience and adaptive coping, while adverse experiences may disrupt development-though their effects are not always permanent and can be mitigated by later supportive environments.

Development is therefore best understood as a **dynamic, reciprocal process** . Biology influences how individuals respond to their environments, while environments and experiences can alter brain functioning and psychological patterns over time. This interactive perspective explains individual differences in development and reinforces that human growth is flexible, context-sensitive, and shaped by ongoing interaction rather than predetermined by any single factor.

Psychological development arises from the continuous interaction of **biological factors, environmental conditions, and lived experiences** , rather than from any single source acting alone. Biology provides the initial framework for development through genetic inheritance, brain structure, and physiological maturation. These biological elements influence basic tendencies such as emotional sensitivity, learning capacity, and behavioural style. However, they do not operate in isolation or dictate fixed outcomes.

The environment plays a decisive role in shaping how biological potentials unfold. Family relationships, cultural practices, schooling, peer interactions, and broader social conditions influence thinking patterns, emotional expression, and behaviour. Supportive environments can encourage curiosity, confidence, and emotional stability, while adverse or restrictive settings may limit growth or create psychological strain. Culture, in particular, guides values, communication styles, and expectations, giving meaning to individual behaviour and emotions.

1.3 Theoretical Perspectives on Development

Developmental psychology draws upon multiple theoretical frameworks to explain age-related change. Cognitive theories emphasize how thinking evolves, psychosocial approaches focus on emotional and social challenges, and learning theories highlight experience and reinforcement.

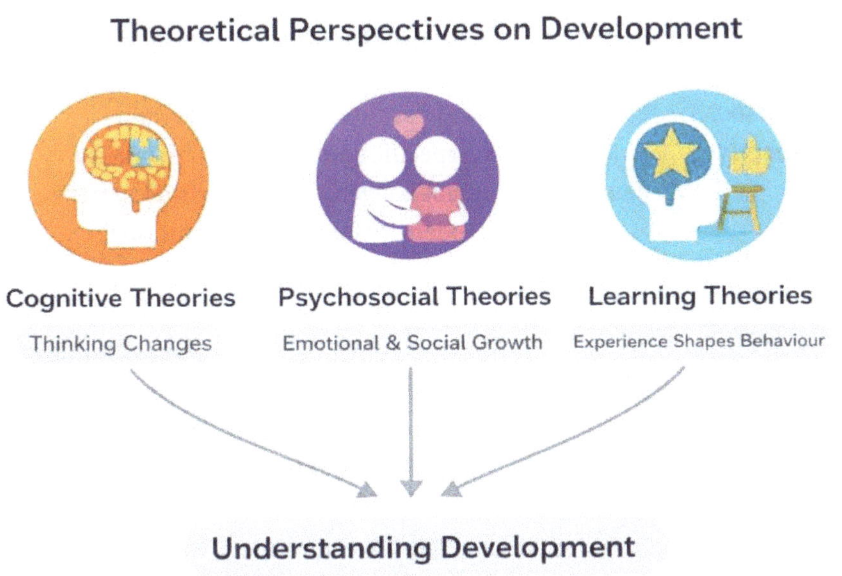

Theoretical Perspectives on Development provide structured ways to understand how psychological change occurs across different stages of life. Because human development is complex, no single theory can fully explain how thinking, emotion, and behaviour evolve with age. Developmental psychology therefore relies on multiple perspectives, each emphasizing different but complementary aspects of growth.

Theoretical Perspective	Primary Focus	Key Developmental Emphasis	Contribution to Lifespan Understanding
Cognitive Perspective	Thinking and reasoning processes	Explains how mental abilities progress from concrete understanding to abstract and reflective reasoning across age	Clarifies age-related changes in learning, problem-solving, memory, and decision-making
Psychosocial Perspective	Emotional and social development	Focuses on age-specific emotional challenges, identity formation, and social relationships	Explains personality development, emotional maturity, and social adaptation across life stages
Learning Perspective	Experience and behaviour	Emphasizes the role of reinforcement, observation, and environmental interaction	Accounts for individual differences and shows how experiences shape behaviour and emotional responses
Biological Perspective	Maturation and brain development	Highlights genetic influences and neurological growth	Provides the foundation for understanding age-related capacities and limitations

Integrative Lifespan Approach	Interaction of multiple factors	Combines cognitive, emotional, social, and experiential influences	Offers a holistic explanation of how development continues and adapts throughout life

Cognitive theories focus on changes in thinking, reasoning, and problem-solving abilities over time. These approaches explain how individuals move from simple, concrete ways of understanding the world to more abstract, logical, and reflective forms of thought. Cognitive perspectives help clarify age-related shifts in learning capacity, memory, decision-making, and intellectual flexibility, showing how mental processes mature and adapt with experience.

Psychosocial theories emphasize emotional development and social relationships at different life stages. They examine how individuals face age-specific challenges related to identity, intimacy, responsibility, and meaning. From this viewpoint, development involves resolving emotional and social tasks shaped by family roles, cultural expectations, and life transitions. Psychosocial theories explain how personality, self-concept, and emotional well-being evolve as people navigate changing social demands across the lifespan.

Learning theories highlight the role of experience, observation, and reinforcement in shaping behaviour and emotional responses. These perspectives stress that development is strongly influenced by interaction with the environment. Behaviours, coping styles, and emotional reactions are learned through rewards, consequences, and social modelling. Learning-based approaches help explain individual differences, showing how similar biological capacities can lead to different outcomes depending on experiences.

Together, these theoretical perspectives create a **comprehensive framework** for understanding development. Cognitive theories explain how thinking changes, psychosocial theories illuminate emotional and social growth, and learning theories reveal how experience shapes behaviour. When combined, they offer a holistic view of how age reshapes mental and emotional functioning throughout the entire lifespan.

1.4 Cognitive and Emotional Change Across Age

As individuals age, their thinking abilities and emotional responses undergo predictable yet individualized changes. Early life is marked by rapid learning and emotional dependence, while later stages involve reflection, emotional balance, and meaning-making.

Cognitive and Emotional Change Across Age refers to the gradual transformation of how individuals think, understand, and manage emotions as they move through different stages of life. In early childhood, cognition is closely tied to immediate perception and sensory experience. Learning occurs rapidly, but thinking is often concrete and dependent on direct interaction with the environment. Emotionally, young children rely heavily on caregivers for security and regulation, expressing feelings openly and learning control through guidance and modelling.

During adolescence and early adulthood, cognitive abilities expand significantly. Individuals develop the capacity for abstract reasoning, critical thinking, and hypothetical problem-solving. This period is marked by exploration, identity formation, and heightened emotional intensity. While emotional experiences may be strong and sometimes unstable, individuals gradually learn to reflect on their feelings and consider multiple perspectives. Social relationships and personal experiences play a key role in shaping both cognitive growth and emotional awareness during this stage.

In middle adulthood, thinking becomes more integrative and experience-based. Individuals often combine logic with practical knowledge, allowing them to navigate complex personal and professional situations effectively. Emotionally, there is typically greater stability and self-control. People become more skilled at regulating emotions, prioritizing meaningful relationships, and coping with stress through learned strategies.

Later adulthood is characterized by reflection, life review, and meaning-making. Although some cognitive processes such as processing speed may slow, accumulated knowledge and wisdom often compensate. Emotional development in this stage emphasizes balance, acceptance, and resilience. Older adults tend to manage emotions more effectively, focusing on emotional well-being and purposeful engagement. Overall, cognitive and emotional development across age reflects a continuous process of adaptation, growth, and refinement shaped by both maturation and experience.

Multiple Choice Questions (MCQs)

1. Human development is best understood as a process that:

A. Ends with physical maturity in adolescence
B. Occurs only during childhood and early adulthood
C. Continues from birth through old age
D. Remains unchanged after early experiences

Correct Answer: C

2. Which statement best reflects the interactionist view of development?

A. Genetics alone determine psychological outcomes
B. Environment overrides all biological influences
C. Development results from biology, environment, and experience

acting together

D. Learning is independent of biological maturation

Correct Answer: C

3. As individuals move from childhood to adulthood, cognitive development typically involves:

A. A decline in learning ability

B. A shift from abstract to concrete thinking

C. Progression from concrete thinking to abstract reasoning

D. Elimination of emotional influence on thinking

Correct Answer: C

4. Emotional development across the lifespan is generally characterized by:

A. Increasing emotional instability with age

B. Complete emotional dependence in adulthood

C. Gradual improvement in emotional regulation and resilience

D. Lack of change after adolescence

Correct Answer: C

5. Why are multiple theoretical perspectives necessary to understand human development?

A. Each theory explains only childhood development

B. Development is too random to be explained by a single framework

C. Different theories highlight complementary aspects of psychological growth

D. Biological theories are insufficient and should be ignored

Correct Answer: C

Short-Answer Questions

1. What is meant by human development as a lifelong process?
2. How do biological and environmental factors interact in psychological development?
3. Mention two cognitive changes that typically occur with increasing age.
4. Why is emotional regulation considered an important outcome of development?
5. State the role of experience in shaping individual development.
6. How does viewing development as dynamic challenge the idea that personality traits are fixed early in life?

Long-Answer Questions

1. Explain human development as a continuous process across the lifespan, highlighting changes in cognition and emotion at different stages of life.
2. Discuss the interaction of biology, environment, and experience in shaping psychological development, using suitable examples.
3. Describe how cognitive abilities and emotional responses change from early childhood to later adulthood.

4. Examine the major theoretical perspectives on human development and explain how they collectively contribute to understanding age-related change.
5. Analyse why development cannot be explained by a single factor and justify the need for an integrative lifespan approach.

2

The Infant Mind – Foundations of Perception and Attachment

2.1 Early Sensory and Perceptual Development

Infancy is characterized by rapid sensory and perceptual growth. Newborns actively process sights, sounds, touch, and movement, gradually organizing these inputs into meaningful experiences. Early perception lays the groundwork for later cognition, as infants begin to recognize patterns, faces, and familiar voices.

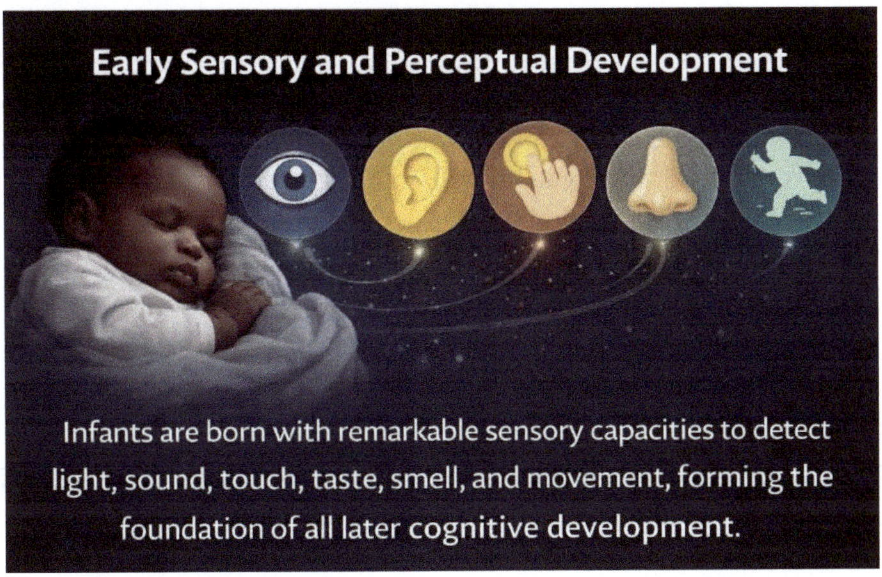

Early sensory and perceptual development forms the foundation of human psychological growth, beginning immediately at birth. Infancy is a period of intense neurological activity, during which the brain rapidly organizes sensory input from the environment. Newborns are not passive recipients of stimulation; rather, they actively attend to and interpret sensory information such as light, sound, touch, taste, smell, and bodily movement. Although their sensory systems are still immature, infants possess remarkable capacities to detect contrasts, rhythms, and patterns that help them make sense of their surroundings.

Visual perception develops progressively during the first year of life. While newborns initially perceive the world in blurred outlines, they show a clear preference for human faces and high-contrast shapes. Over time, improvements in visual acuity and depth perception allow infants to track moving objects, distinguish colours, and recognize familiar people. This growing visual sensitivity supports emotional bonding, particularly through eye contact and facial expressions, which play a crucial role in early social development.

Auditory perception is comparatively well developed at birth. Infants can distinguish between different speech sounds and show sensitivity to the rhythm and tone of human voices. They often respond more strongly to familiar voices, especially those heard repeatedly before birth, such as a caregiver's voice. This early auditory discrimination prepares infants for later language acquisition by tuning their perception to speech patterns long before they can speak.

Tactile and proprioceptive senses also contribute significantly to early perception. Through touch, movement, and bodily sensations, infants learn about the physical properties of objects and their own bodies. Grasping, sucking, and exploratory movements help integrate sensory experiences with motor actions. These interactions support the development of body awareness and coordination, which are essential for later skills such as crawling, walking, and purposeful manipulation of objects.

Overall, early sensory and perceptual development serves as the groundwork for higher cognitive processes. By organizing raw sensory input into coherent experiences, infants begin to form expectations, recognize familiar stimuli, and respond meaningfully to their environment. This early perceptual organization enables learning, social engagement, and adaptive behaviour well before the emergence of language, demonstrating that cognition begins through perception in the earliest stages of life.

2.2 Emotional Expression in Infancy

Infants communicate emotions primarily through facial expressions, crying, and body movements. Basic emotional states such as pleasure, distress, and interest appear early, while more complex emotions develop later.

Emotional expression in infancy represents one of the earliest forms of human communication and plays a vital role in survival, attachment, and psychological development. Since infants lack verbal language, they rely on nonverbal signals-such as facial expressions, crying, vocal sounds, and body movements-to convey their internal states. These expressions allow infants to signal comfort, discomfort, curiosity, or need, ensuring timely responses from caregivers.

Basic emotional expressions emerge early in life. Feelings such as pleasure, distress, and interest are evident within the first few months. Smiling often reflects contentment or social engagement, while crying serves as a powerful signal of hunger, pain, fatigue, or emotional discomfort. Body movements-such as kicking, arching, or reaching-further communicate excitement, frustration, or a desire for interaction. These early emotions are largely reflexive but gradually become more differentiated as the infant gains neurological and experiential maturity.

As infancy progresses, emotional expression becomes more organized and socially responsive. Infants begin to show joy during playful interactions, discomfort in unfamiliar situations, and calmness in the presence of trusted caregivers. Although complex emotions such as shame, guilt, or pride develop later and require self-awareness, the foundations for these emotions are laid during infancy through repeated emotional exchanges. Responsive caregiving helps infants learn that emotions can be expressed, understood, and regulated within relationships.

Emotional expression in infancy also plays a crucial role in bonding and attachment. When caregivers respond sensitively to an infant's emotional signals, a sense of security and trust develops. These early emotional interactions help infants form expectations about relationships, influencing how they later perceive, express, and manage emotions. Consistent emotional responsiveness fosters emotional awareness and resilience, while neglect or misstatement may disrupt emotional development.

2.3 Attachment and Emotional Security

Attachment refers to the emotional bond between an infant and primary caregiver. Secure attachment develops when caregivers respond consistently and sensitively to an infant's needs. According to John Bowlby, early attachment experiences create internal emotional frameworks that influence trust, relationships, and emotional regulation throughout life.

Attachment refers to the deep and enduring emotional bond that develops between an infant and a primary caregiver, forming the foundation of emotional security. This bond is not simply based on physical care but on the quality of emotional responsiveness provided to the infant. When caregivers respond consistently, promptly, and sensitively to an infant's signals-such as crying, smiling, or reaching-the child begins to experience the world as safe and predictable. This sense of security supports healthy emotional and social development.

Secure attachment develops through repeated interactions in which the caregiver meets the infant's physical and emotional needs. For example, comforting an infant when they are distressed, responding warmly to social cues, and providing reassurance in unfamiliar situations help the infant regulate emotions. Over time, the infant internalizes these experiences, learning that support is available during moments of stress. This emotional safety allows the child to explore their environment confidently, knowing they can return to a trusted caregiver when needed.

The theoretical foundation of attachment is strongly associated with the work of John Bowlby, who emphasized that early attachment relationships shape internal emotional frameworks, often referred to as internal working models. These models influence how individuals perceive themselves and others, guiding expectations about trust, care, and emotional availability. A securely attached child is more likely to develop healthy self-esteem, effective emotional regulation, and positive interpersonal relationships later in life.

In contrast, insecure attachment may develop when caregiving is inconsistent, unresponsive, or emotionally unavailable. Infants in such environments may struggle to predict caregiver behaviour, leading to heightened anxiety, emotional withdrawal, or difficulty regulating distress. These early patterns can persist, increasing vulnerability to emotional difficulties, relationship challenges, or reduced coping abilities in later childhood and adulthood.

Overall, attachment and emotional security formed in infancy play a crucial role in shaping lifelong emotional functioning. Early caregiving experiences do not rigidly determine future outcomes, but they significantly influence how individuals manage emotions, form relationships, and respond to stress across the lifespan.

2.4 Early Brain Development and Learning

Infancy is a critical period for brain development, marked by rapid neural growth and synaptic connections. Experiences such as touch, sound, and caregiver interaction actively shape brain architecture. Learning during infancy occurs through exploration, imitation, and repetition.

Early brain development during infancy is marked by extraordinary growth and plasticity, making this period crucial for lifelong learning and development. At birth, the infant's brain contains billions of neurons, but the connections between them-known as synapses-are still forming. During the first few years of life, neural connections multiply rapidly in response to experiences, allowing the brain to adapt to environmental demands. This rapid synaptic growth enables infants to acquire foundational cognitive, emotional, and motor abilities.

Experiences play a central role in shaping brain architecture. Sensory inputs such as touch, sound, sight, and movement stimulate neural activity, strengthening frequently used connections while unused ones gradually fade. Interactions with caregivers-such as talking, holding, playing, and responding to emotional cues-are especially influential. These interactions not only support language and cognitive development but also help organize brain systems involved in emotion regulation and social understanding.

Learning in infancy occurs primarily through active engagement with the environment. Infants learn by exploring objects, observing people, imitating actions, and repeating behaviours that produce interesting or rewarding outcomes. Simple activities such as reaching for toys, babbling sounds, or copying facial expressions help infants understand cause-and-effect relationships. Through repetition, neural pathways become more efficient, forming the basis for memory, attention, and critical thinking skills.

Positive stimulation during this period enhances both cognitive and emotional capacities. Environments rich in warmth, responsiveness, and varied sensory experiences promote healthy brain development and curiosity-driven learning. Conversely, deprivation-such as lack of stimulation, neglect, or limited social interaction-can disrupt neural development. Prolonged absence of supportive experiences may weaken cognitive growth and emotional resilience, highlighting the importance of early nurturing environments.

Aspect of Development	Key Characteristics	Role in Learning	Long-Term Impact
Neural Growth	Rapid increase in neurons and synaptic connections during infancy	Supports quick processing of sensory information	Forms the biological foundation for cognition and behaviour
Sensory Stimulation	Exposure to touch, sound, sight, and movement	Activates and strengthens neural pathways	Enhances perception, attention, and responsiveness
Caregiver Interaction	Responsive talking, holding, and emotional engagement	Facilitates social learning and emotional regulation	Promotes secure attachment and emotional stability
Exploration	Manipulating objects and observing surroundings	Encourages curiosity and discovery-based learning	Develops problem-solving and adaptive skills
Imitation	Copying sounds, gestures, and facial expressions	Supports early communication and social learning	Lays groundwork for language and social competence
Repetition	Repeated actions and experiences	Reinforces neural connections	Strengthens memory and learning efficiency
Positive Stimulation	Warm, enriched, and supportive environments	Accelerates cognitive and emotional development	Builds resilience and lifelong learning capacity

Multiple Choice Questions (MCQs)

1. Which of the following best describes sensory and perceptual development in infancy?

A. Infants are passive receivers of sensory input

B. Sensory abilities are fully mature at birth

C. Infants actively process sensory information from birth

D. Perception begins only after language development

Answer: C

2. Which sense is relatively well developed at birth compared to others?

A. Visual perception

B. Auditory perception

C. Depth perception

D. Colour discrimination

Answer: B

3. The primary way infants communicate emotional states is through:

A. Spoken language

B. Written symbols

C. Nonverbal expressions and crying

D. Logical reasoning

Answer: C

4. According to attachment theory, secure attachment develops when caregivers:

A. Encourage early independence

B. Respond consistently and sensitively to infant needs

C. Limit physical contact

D. Maintain strict discipline

Answer: B

5. Why is infancy considered a critical period for brain development?

A. Brain development stops after infancy

B. Learning occurs only through formal education

C. Neural connections rapidly form and are shaped by experience

D. Cognitive abilities are fixed at birth

Answer: C

Short Answer Questions

1. What is meant by sensory and perceptual development in infancy?
2. How do infants express basic emotions before language develops?
3. Define attachment in the context of infant emotional development.
4. Why are caregiver–infant interactions important during early brain development?
5. What role does repetition play in learning during infancy?

6. How do early sensory experiences influence an infant's interaction with the environment?

Long Answer Questions

1. Explain how early sensory and perceptual experiences contribute to cognitive development in infancy.
2. Discuss the significance of emotional expression in infancy and its role in communication and survival.
3. Examine the concept of attachment and explain how secure attachment promotes emotional security.
4. Analyse the role of early brain plasticity in shaping learning and behaviour during infancy.
5. "Early experiences influence, but do not rigidly determine, later development." Discuss this statement with reference to infancy and attachment.
6. Discuss how emotional responsiveness from caregivers supports emotional regulation and learning during infancy.

3

Early Childhood – Language, Imagination, and Emotional Growth

3.1 Language Development and Thought Formation

Early childhood is marked by dramatic growth in language abilities. Children move from single words to complex sentences, enabling more advanced thinking and communication. Language not only facilitates social interaction but also reshapes cognitive processes such as memory, planning, and problem-solving.

Early childhood represents a pivotal phase in which language growth and cognitive development become deeply interconnected. During this period, children progress from using isolated words to forming structured phrases and eventually grammatically organized sentences. This rapid expansion in vocabulary and syntax allows them to express needs, describe objects, and communicate ideas with increasing precision. As children gain linguistic competence, their ability to interact meaningfully with caregivers and peers also strengthens, laying the foundation for social learning.

Language development does more than support communication; it actively shapes how children think. Through words, children learn to categorize experiences, organize information, and make sense of the world around them. Naming objects, actions, and relationships helps them form mental representations, which in turn improves memory and conceptual understanding. For example, a child who can verbally label shapes or colours is better able to recall and compare them during problem-solving tasks. Language thus becomes a cognitive tool that supports reasoning, planning, and decision-making.

An important outcome of language growth is the emergence of self-directed speech. Young children often talk aloud while playing or attempting tasks, using language to guide their actions. This form of speech gradually becomes internalized as inner speech, enabling children to plan steps, regulate behaviour, and evaluate outcomes mentally. Such internal dialogue is essential for developing self-control and independent critical thinking skills.

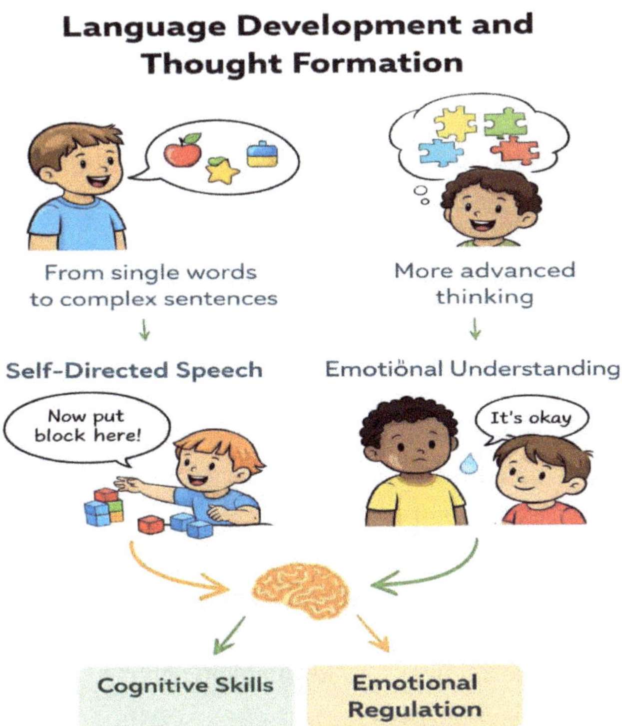

Language also plays a crucial role in emotional understanding. By learning words for feelings such as happiness, anger, or fear, children gain the ability to recognize and communicate their emotional states. This verbal labelling supports emotional regulation, as children can express distress through words rather than behaviour alone. Overall, the development of language in early childhood not only enhances communication but fundamentally transforms thought processes, contributing to cognitive, emotional, and social growth.

Aspect of Emotional Development	Early Childhood Characteristics	Role of Adults (Caregivers/Teachers)	Long-Term Outcomes
Emotional Awareness	Children begin to recognize basic emotions such as happiness, anger, fear, and sadness	Label emotions verbally and help children identify feelings	Improved emotional understanding and self-awareness
Emotional Expression	Emotions often expressed through crying, tantrums, or excitement	Encourage verbal expression and appropriate emotional responses	Reduced impulsive behaviour and healthier expression of feelings
Emotional Regulation	Limited self-control; difficulty managing frustration and delay	Teach coping strategies such as calming techniques and problem-solving	Better self-regulation and stress management skills
Social–Emotional Interaction	Emotions strongly influenced by peer interactions and situations	Model empathy, patience, and constructive conflict resolution	Stronger social relationships and cooperation

3.2 Imagination and Symbolic Thinking

Imagination flourishes during early childhood as children engage in pretend play and symbolic representation. Objects, actions, and words are used to represent ideas beyond immediate reality. This form of thinking supports creativity, emotional expression, and social understanding.

Early childhood is a stage in which imagination expands rapidly, allowing children to move beyond literal interpretations of the world. During this period, children begin to engage in symbolic thinking-the ability to let one thing stand for another. Everyday objects may take on new meanings, such as a stick becoming a sword or a box turning into a house. This capacity to detach meaning from physical reality marks an important cognitive shift and reflects growing mental flexibility.

Imagination is most clearly expressed through pretend play. When children invent scenarios, characters, and storylines, they are not merely entertaining themselves; they are actively constructing and testing ideas about how the world works. Pretend play enables children to rehearse real-life situations, experiment with problem-solving strategies, and explore possibilities that may not be immediately available to them. In doing so, they learn to think creatively and adaptively.

Symbolic thinking also plays a vital role in emotional development. By acting out experiences or emotions in imaginative play, children find safe ways to express feelings such as fear, excitement, jealousy, or empathy. For example, playing the role of a caregiver or hero allows a child to process emotions related to power, responsibility, or care. This imaginative expression helps children make sense of their inner experiences and gradually develop emotional regulation.

Social understanding is further strengthened through imagination. When children take on different roles-such as a parent, teacher, or friend-they begin to see situations from perspectives other than their own. This role-taking encourages empathy, cooperation, and an early sense of morality. Through symbolic and imaginative play, children explore rules, fairness, and relationships, making imagination a crucial bridge between cognitive growth, emotional awareness, and social competence in early childhood.

3.3 Emotional Awareness and Regulation

Children gradually learn to identify, express, and manage emotions during early childhood. Emotional outbursts become more controlled as cognitive and language skills improve. Guidance from caregivers and teachers plays a crucial role in teaching children how to cope with frustration, fear, and excitement.

Emotional awareness and regulation develop progressively during early childhood as children become more conscious of their internal emotional states. At a young age, emotions are often expressed in raw and immediate ways, such as crying, tantrums, or laughter, because children have limited ability to understand or control their feelings. As cognitive and language abilities mature, children begin to recognize different emotions, understand their causes, and express them more clearly through words rather than impulsive actions.

Language development plays a critical role in emotional regulation. When children learn to name emotions like anger, sadness, fear, or excitement, they gain tools to communicate distress and seek support. Verbal expression helps reduce emotional overload, allowing children to pause, reflect, and choose more appropriate responses. For example, a child who can say "I am angry" is better equipped to manage frustration than one who can only express it through aggressive behaviour.

Emotional regulation is also strongly influenced by adult guidance. Caregivers and teachers model appropriate emotional responses and provide consistent support when children experience strong feelings. Through reassurance, explanation, and gentle discipline, adults instruct children coping strategies such as deep breathing, taking turns, or waiting patiently. These interactions help children learn that emotions are manageable and that difficult feelings do not have to result in loss of control.

Over time, children internalize these regulatory strategies, leading to greater self-control and emotional resilience. The ability to manage emotions effectively during early childhood is linked to later mental health, social competence, and academic adjustment. Children who develop healthy emotional regulation skills are more likely to form positive relationships, handle stress constructively, and adapt successfully to future challenges, making this stage a critical foundation for lifelong emotional well-being.

3.4 Social Interaction and Self-Concept

As social exposure expands beyond the family, children develop a sense of self shaped by feedback from others. Peer interactions help children learn cooperation, empathy, and conflict resolution. Early successes and failures contribute to emerging self-esteem and confidence.

During early childhood, children's social worlds broaden as they interact more frequently with peers, teachers, and individuals outside the immediate family. These expanding interactions play a central role in shaping the child's self-concept-the understanding of who they are, what they can do, and how they are valued by others. Children begin to see themselves not only through their own experiences but also through the responses, reactions, and feedback they receive from people around them.

Peer interaction is especially influential at this stage. Through play, group activities, and shared tasks, children learn essential social skills such as cooperation, sharing, turn-taking, and empathy. Conflicts with peers, though sometimes challenging, provide valuable learning opportunities. By navigating disagreements, children gradually understand perspectives other than their own and learn constructive ways to resolve problems. These experiences help them develop emotional sensitivity and social awareness.

Social experiences also contribute directly to the formation of self-esteem. Positive interactions-such as being included in play, praised for effort, or supported during difficulties-strengthen a child's sense of competence and self-worth. Conversely, repeated experiences of rejection or criticism may lead to self-doubt or withdrawal. Early successes and failures therefore become meaningful reference points through which children evaluate their abilities and social value.

A supportive and nurturing social environment is crucial for healthy self-concept development. When caregivers and educators provide encouragement, model respectful behaviour, and create inclusive settings, children are more likely to develop confidence and adaptive social behaviour. Such environments help children feel secure, valued, and capable, forming a strong emotional and social foundation that supports well-being, resilience, and positive relationships later in life.

ocial Interaction and the Architecture of the Self

As social exposure expands beyond the family, children develop a sense of self shaped by feedback from others. Peer interactions help children learn cooperation, empathy, and conflict resolution. Early successes and failures contribute to emerging self-esteem and confidence. During early childhood, children's social worlds broaden as they interact more frequently with peers, teachers, and individuals outside the immediate family. These expanding interactions play a central role in shaping the child's **self-concept**—the understanding of who they are, what they can do, and how they are valued by others.

Children begin to see themselves not only through their own experiences but also through the responses, reactions, and feedback they receive from people around them. This phenomenon is often described in sociology and psychology as the "**Looking-Glass Self.**" In this process, the child uses the social world as a mirror; if the "mirror" reflects back a person who is helpful, funny, or capable, the child internalizes these labels as core truths about their identity.

The Shift from Egocentrism to Empathy

Peer interaction is especially influential at this stage. Through play, group activities, and shared tasks, children learn essential social skills such as cooperation, sharing, turn-taking, and empathy. This transition marks a significant cognitive milestone: the move away from **egocentrism**. While toddlers believe everyone sees the world exactly as they do, school-age children begin to develop a **"Theory of Mind."** They start to realize that a friend might feel sad even if they themselves are happy, or that a peer might have a different reason for wanting a specific toy.

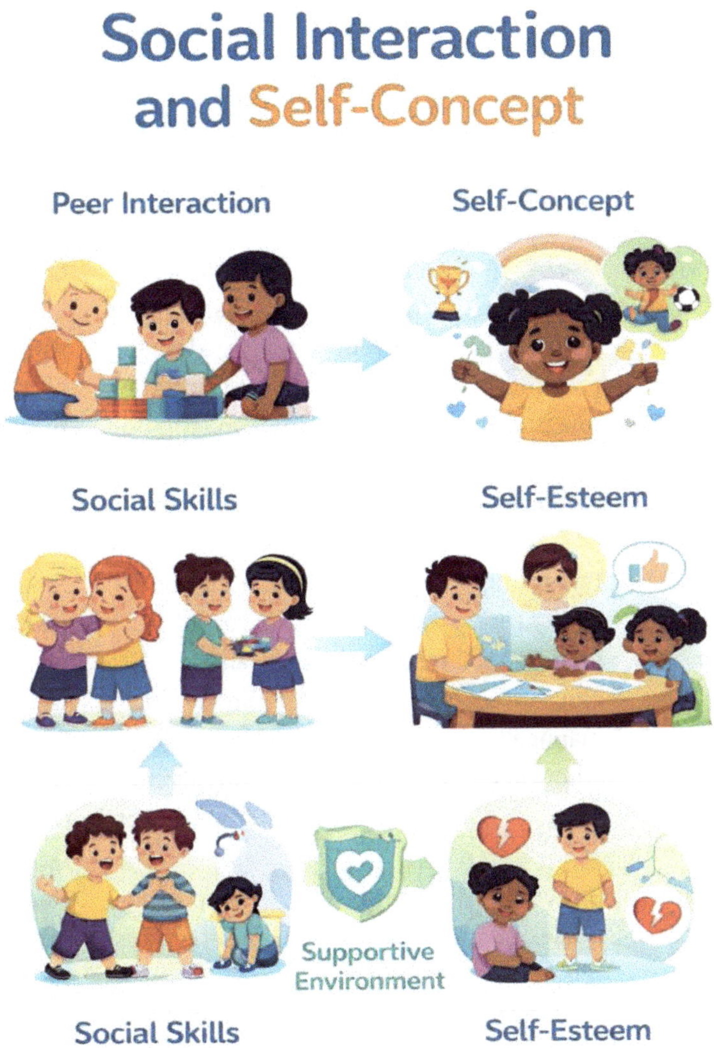

Dimension	Core Features	Key Developmental Processes	Role of Environment	Long-Term Significance
3.1 Language Development and Thought Formation	Rapid growth from single words to complex sentences	Language shapes memory, planning, problem-solving, and reflective thinking	Rich verbal interaction with adults and peers	Enhanced cognitive flexibility, reasoning ability, and emotional articulation
3.2 Imagination and Symbolic Thinking	Use of symbols, pretend play, and imaginative scenarios	Objects and actions represent abstract ideas beyond immediate reality	Play-based learning and freedom to explore imagination	Creativity, abstract thinking, moral reasoning, and social perspective-taking
3.3 Emotional Awareness and Regulation	Increasing ability to identify and manage emotions	Shift from impulsive outbursts to controlled emotional responses	Emotional coaching and modelling by caregivers and teachers	Emotional resilience, mental well-being, and adaptive coping skills
3.4 Social Interaction and Self-Concept	Growing sense of self influenced	Learning cooperation, empathy, conflict resolution,	Supportive peer groups and inclusive social	Healthy self-esteem, confidence, and

	by social feedback	and self-evaluation	environmen ts	positive social behaviour

Multiple Choice Questions (MCQs)

1. Which developmental change best characterizes language growth in early childhood?

A. Shift from gestures to reflexive sounds

B. Transition from single words to complex sentences

C. Decline in vocabulary use

D. Replacement of speech by symbolic gestures

Answer: B

2. How does language development influence cognitive processes in early childhood?

A. It limits creative thinking

B. It replaces emotional expression

C. It reshapes memory, planning, and problem-solving

D. It functions only as a communication tool

Answer: C

3. What is symbolic thinking in early childhood?

A. The ability to memorize symbols without meaning

B. The use of objects or actions to represent ideas beyond immediate reality

C. The preference for logical reasoning over imagination

D. The rejection of pretend play

Answer: B

4. Which activity best supports imagination and social understanding in young children?

A. Rote memorization tasks

B. Passive observation of adults

C. Pretend and role-based play

D. Solitary rule-based games

Answer: C

5. Why is emotional regulation in early childhood important for later development?

A. It reduces the need for social interaction

B. It prevents emotional expression

C. It forms the foundation for mental health and social adjustment

D. It eliminates emotional challenges in adulthood

Answer: C

Short Answer Questions

1. What role does language play in shaping thinking during early childhood?
2. Define symbolic thinking with reference to early childhood development.
3. How does pretend play contribute to emotional expression in children?
4. What is meant by emotional regulation in early childhood?

5. How do peer interactions influence a child's self-concept?
6. How does self-directed speech contribute to the development of self-control and independent behavior in early childhood?

Long Answer Questions

1. Explain how language development during early childhood transforms cognitive processes such as memory, planning, and problem-solving.
2. Discuss the significance of imagination and symbolic thinking in the social and emotional development of young children.
3. Analyse the process through which children learn emotional awareness and regulation, highlighting the role of caregivers and teachers.
4. Examine how social interactions beyond the family shape self-concept and self-esteem in early childhood.
5. "A supportive environment is essential for healthy emotional growth in early childhood." Justify this statement with suitable examples.
6. Discuss how language development, imaginative play, emotional regulation, and social interaction collectively contribute to the holistic development of a child's self-concept during early childhood.

4

Middle Childhood – Reasoning, Morality, and Social Awareness

4.1 Development of Logical and Structured Thinking

Middle childhood marks a significant shift from intuitive thought to more organized and logical reasoning. Children become capable of understanding cause–effect relationships, classification, and basic problem-solving.

During middle childhood, children undergo a noticeable transformation in how they think and reason. Their thought processes gradually move away from reliance on guesswork, perception, or immediate impressions and become more organized, deliberate, and logical. At this stage, children are better able to understand clear relationships between actions and outcomes, helping them recognize that events occur for specific reasons rather than by chance. This growing awareness of cause and effect allows them to predict consequences and make more thoughtful choices.

Children also develop the ability to classify objects, ideas, and information into meaningful categories based on shared characteristics. For example, they can group items by size, function, or type and understand that an object can belong to more than one category at the same time. Such classification skills support mathematical reasoning, reading comprehension, and scientific thinking, as children learn to organize information in structured ways.

Another important change is the reduction of egocentric thinking. Children become more capable of considering viewpoints other than their own and are increasingly guided by rules and logical principles. They learn to follow instructions, apply step-by-step strategies, and solve problems systematically rather than through trial and error. This shift enables them to approach academic tasks with greater concentration and consistency.

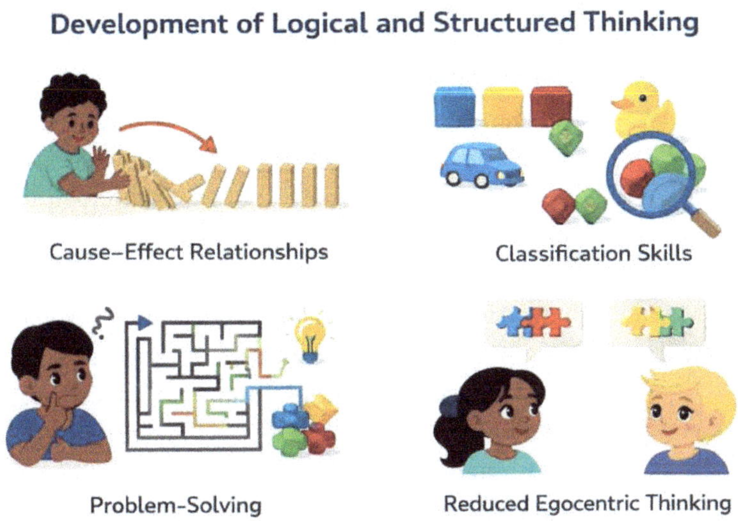

Overall, the development of logical and structured thinking during middle childhood strengthens both learning and everyday decision-making. Children become more confident analytical people who can analyse situations, apply rules, and think through challenges in a rational manner, laying a strong foundation for advanced reasoning in later stages of development.

4.2 Moral Understanding and Rule Awareness

During this stage, children develop a clearer sense of right and wrong, moving beyond blind obedience to rules toward understanding intentions and fairness. Moral reasoning becomes more nuanced as children consider social norms, consequences, and peer expectations.

During middle childhood, children show marked progress in how they understand rules, morality, and social expectations. Rather than viewing rules as fixed commands imposed by adults, they begin to recognize that rules serve purposes such as maintaining fairness, safety, and cooperation.

This shift reflects a deeper moral awareness in which children evaluate actions not only by outcomes but also by the intentions behind them.

Aspect	Early Childhood	Middle Childhood	Key Developmental Significance
View of Rules	Rules are seen as fixed and imposed by adults	Rules are understood as flexible and socially agreed upon	Shows shift from blind obedience to thoughtful rule interpretation
Basis of Moral Judgment	Judged mainly by consequences (e.g., punishment)	Judged by intentions, fairness, and context	Indicates more mature and nuanced moral reasoning
Role of Authority	Adult authority is primary	Peers and mutual agreement gain importance	Reflects growing independence from external control
Understanding of Fairness	Limited and self-centred	Emphasis on equality, fairness, and reciprocity	Supports cooperative behaviour and social harmony
Influence of Social Interaction	Minimal peer influence	Strong peer interaction and negotiation	Helps internalize social norms and values
Alignment with Theory	Heteronomous morality	Autonomous morality	Consistent with Jean Piaget's theory of moral development

At this stage, moral reasoning becomes more flexible and context-sensitive. Children start to understand that the same rule may be applied differently depending on the situation. For instance, they may judge an action less harshly if it was accidental rather than intentional. This growing sensitivity to intention indicates an important cognitive advancement, as children move beyond rigid thinking toward balanced moral judgments.

Social interaction plays a crucial role in shaping moral understanding. Peer relationships expose children to negotiation, conflict, and cooperation, all of which require consideration of others' perspectives. Through group activities and play, children learn about fairness, equality, and mutual respect. Peer expectations increasingly influence behaviour, sometimes more strongly than adult authority, encouraging children to align their actions with shared group values.

These developments closely align with the ideas of **Jean Piaget**, who described a transition from heteronomous morality-where rules are seen as unchangeable and enforced by authority-to autonomous morality, where children understand that rules are socially constructed and can be modified through agreement. Overall, moral understanding in middle childhood reflects growing independence, empathy, and internalization of ethical values, laying the foundation for mature moral reasoning in adolescence and adulthood.

4.3 Peer Relationships and Social Comparison

Peers play an increasingly central role in emotional and social development during middle childhood. Children compare abilities, appearance, and achievements, shaping self-esteem and identity. Friendships become more stable and based on trust, cooperation, and shared interests. While positive peer relationships foster confidence and belonging, negative experiences such as rejection can affect emotional well-being.

During middle childhood, peer relationships become a major influence on children's emotional, social, and psychological development. Unlike early childhood, where family remains the primary social reference point, children now spend more time with peers in school and group settings. These interactions significantly shape how children view themselves and others. Acceptance, friendship, and group belonging begin to play a central role in emotional security and daily behaviour.

A key feature of this stage is **social comparison** . Children start comparing their abilities, appearance, academic performance, and talents with those of their peers. Such comparisons help them evaluate their strengths and weaknesses, contributing to the development of self-esteem and personal identity. Positive comparisons-such as feeling competent in sports or academics-can enhance confidence, while repeated unfavourable comparisons may lead to self-doubt or feelings of inadequacy.

Friendships during middle childhood also become more stable and meaningful. Children value trust, loyalty, cooperation, and shared interests rather than mere proximity or play convenience. They learn important social skills such as compromise, empathy, conflict resolution, and mutual support. These friendships provide emotional reassurance and a sense of belonging, which are essential for healthy social adjustment.

However, peer relationships can also present emotional challenges. Experiences such as exclusion, teasing, or rejection may negatively affect emotional well-being and self-concept. Children who face persistent peer difficulties may show signs of anxiety, withdrawal, or reduced academic engagement. Overall, peer relationships and social comparison during middle childhood play a critical role in shaping emotional resilience, identity formation, and long-term social competence.

4.4 Emotional Regulation and Academic Self-Concept

Children gain improved control over emotions, learning to manage frustration, anxiety, and disappointment. Emotional regulation is closely tied to academic self-concept, as success or failure in school influences motivation and confidence.

During middle childhood, children show significant improvement in their ability to understand and regulate emotions. They become more capable of controlling emotional reactions such as anger, frustration, anxiety, and disappointment, especially in structured environments like classrooms. Instead of expressing emotions impulsively, children increasingly use strategies such as self-talk, problem-solving, or seeking support to cope with challenging situations. This growing emotional control supports better behaviour, social interaction, and learning engagement.

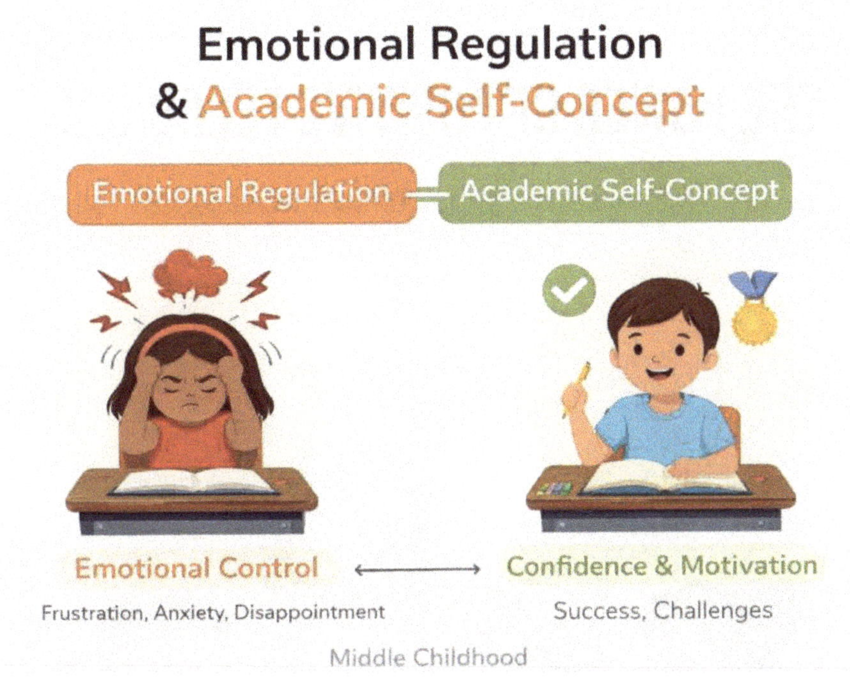

Emotional regulation during this stage is intricately connected to **academic self-concept**, which refers to how children perceive their own abilities and competence in school-related tasks. Success in academics often strengthens confidence, motivation, and willingness to take on new challenges. Conversely, repeated experiences of failure or criticism may lead children to doubt their abilities, increasing anxiety and avoidance of academic tasks. As a result, emotional responses to school experiences play a critical role in shaping how children view themselves as learners.

Feedback from teachers and caregivers strongly influences this process. Supportive, constructive feedback helps children interpret mistakes as opportunities for learning rather than personal shortcomings. When adults emphasize effort, improvement, and persistence instead of only outcomes, children are more likely to develop resilience and a cheerful outlook toward challenges. Such guidance helps children regulate disappointment and maintain motivation even when tasks are difficult.

THE POWER OF POSITIVE FEEDBACK

Mistakes are opportunities to learn.

The development of emotional regulation and academic self-concept during middle childhood lays the foundation for long-term learning attitudes. Children who learn to manage emotions effectively and maintain a balanced view of success and failure are better equipped to handle academic pressure, remain motivated, and approach future challenges with confidence and emotional stability.

Case Study: Emotional Regulation and Academic Self-Concept in Middle Childhood

Background

Ananya, a 10-year-old student in Grade 5, was academically capable but often became anxious during examinations and class presentations. When she made mistakes, she reacted with frustration, sometimes refusing to continue tasks. Although her teachers recognized her potential, her fear of failure and emotional responses began to affect her academic confidence and classroom participation.

Observation and Intervention

Over time, Ananya's teacher and parents worked together to support her emotional regulation. In the classroom, the teacher provided calm, constructive feedback and emphasized effort rather than grades. When Ananya struggled with mathematics problems, she was encouraged to pause, take deep breaths, and break tasks into smaller steps instead of becoming overwhelmed. At home, her parents reinforced the idea that mistakes were a normal part of learning and praised persistence rather than perfection.

Gradually, Ananya learned to manage feelings of anxiety and disappointment more effectively. She began using self-talk such as "I can try again" when facing difficult tasks. After receiving supportive feedback, she became more willing to ask questions and participate in class discussions. Small academic successes further boosted her confidence, helping her associate effort with improvement.

Outcome

By the end of the school term, Ananya demonstrated improved emotional control and a more positive academic self-concept. She approached tests with reduced anxiety, showed greater resilience after setbacks, and displayed increased motivation to learn. Her teachers observed better concentration and sustained effort, even during challenging activities.

Significance

This case study highlights how emotional regulation and academic self-concept are intricately linked in middle childhood. With consistent emotional support and constructive feedback, children can develop resilience, confidence, and a healthier emotional outlook toward academic challenges, enabling long-term success in both learning and emotional well-being.

Multiple Choice Questions (MCQs)

1. Which cognitive change is most characteristic of middle childhood?

A. Thinking based mainly on imagination

B. Reliance on trial-and-error learning

C. Development of logical and structured reasoning

D. Complete abstract thinking

Answer: C

2. During middle childhood, children begin to judge moral actions primarily based on:

A. Fear of punishment

B. Obedience to adult authority

C. Intentions and fairness

D. Cultural traditions alone

Answer: C

3. According to Jean Piaget, the shift toward understanding rules as flexible and socially agreed reflects:

A. Egocentric thinking

B. Heteronomous morality

C. Autonomous morality

D. Preoperational thought

Answer: C

4. Social comparison during middle childhood mainly influences a child:

A. Physical growth

B. Self-esteem and identity

C. Language acquisition

D. Motor coordination

Answer: B

5. Supportive feedback from teachers and caregivers during middle childhood primarily helps children develop:

A. Dependence on authority

B. Avoidance of challenges

C. Emotional regulation and resilience

D. Competitive behaviour only

Answer: C

Short Answer Questions

1. What is meant by logical and structured thinking in middle childhood?
2. How does moral understanding change during middle childhood compared to early childhood?
3. What role do peer relationships play in shaping self-esteem during middle childhood?
4. Define social comparison and explain why it becomes important at this stage.
5. What is emotional regulation, and how does it develop in middle childhood?
6. How does academic self-concept influence a child's motivation to learn?

Long Answer Questions

1. Explain the development of logical reasoning abilities in middle childhood and discuss how these abilities support academic learning and everyday decision-making.
2. Discuss the shift in moral reasoning during middle childhood with reference to rule awareness, intentions, and fairness, drawing on ideas associated with **Jean Piaget**.
3. Analyse the importance of peer relationships in middle childhood, highlighting both positive and negative influences on emotional and social development.
4. Examine how social comparison affects self-esteem and identity formation during middle childhood.
5. Discuss the relationship between emotional regulation and academic self-concept, explaining how success and failure in school influence children's emotional development.

5

Adolescence – Identity Formation and Emotional Intensity

5.1 Cognitive Expansion and Abstract Thinking

Adolescence introduces advanced cognitive abilities, including abstract reasoning, hypothetical thinking, and self-reflection. Teenagers can analyse complex ideas, question assumptions, and consider future possibilities.

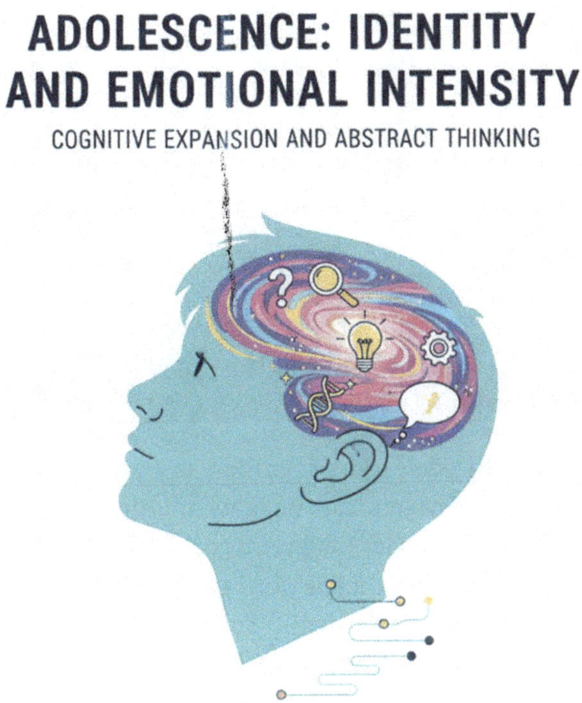

Adolescence represents a major turning point in cognitive development, marked by a shift from concrete, experience-based thinking to more abstract and flexible forms of reasoning. During this stage, individuals begin to think beyond what is immediately visible or directly experienced. They can understand concepts such as justice, freedom, identity, and possibility, which require mental manipulation of ideas rather than reliance on physical examples. This cognitive expansion enables adolescents to grasp symbolic meanings, detect patterns, and engage with complex academic subjects like algebra, literature, philosophy, and science.

A defining feature of adolescent cognition is **hypothetical and future-oriented thinking**. Teenagers can imagine multiple outcomes, evaluate “what if” scenarios, and plan for long-term goals. This allows them to reflect on potential consequences of their actions and consider alternative paths in education, relationships, and careers. Such thinking supports decision-making and problem-solving, although it is still developing and can be influenced by emotions and social pressures.

Another important development is **self-reflection and metacognition** or thinking about one's own thinking. Adolescents become more aware of their beliefs, strengths, weaknesses, and values. They begin to question ideas presented by parents, teachers, and society, not necessarily to reject them, but to evaluate their validity. This critical questioning supports intellectual independence and the formation of personal worldviews.

However, these advanced cognitive abilities can also bring challenges. Increased awareness of abstract possibilities may lead to overthinking, self-doubt, or confusion, especially when adolescents encounter conflicting ideas or moral dilemmas. The ability to imagine negative outcomes can heighten anxiety, while heightened self-awareness may increase sensitivity to criticism. Despite these challenges, cognitive expansion during adolescence lays the foundation for mature reasoning, ethical judgment, and lifelong intellectual growth.

5.2 Identity Exploration and Self-Definition

A central psychological task of adolescence is forming a coherent sense of identity. Adolescents explore values, beliefs, career goals, and social roles while negotiating independence from family. According to Erik Erikson, this stage involves resolving identity versus role confusion.

A defining psychological challenge of adolescence is the development of a clear and stable sense of identity. During this stage, individuals actively explore who they are and who they want to become. This exploration includes personal values, moral beliefs, career aspirations, gender roles, friendships, and cultural or social affiliations. Adolescents begin to ask deeper questions such as *"What do I believe in?," "What kind of person do I want to be?,"* and *"Where do I fit in society?"* These questions reflect a growing need for self-definition and personal meaning.

As adolescents strive for independence, they gradually renegotiate their relationship with family. While caregivers continue to play an important role, teenagers increasingly rely on peers, role models, and personal experiences to shape their identity. Experimentation is common at this stage-adolescents may try different styles, opinions, academic paths, or social groups as part of understanding themselves. Such exploration is a healthy and necessary process rather than a sign of instability.

Psychologist Erik Erikson described adolescence as the stage of *identity versus role confusion*. According to his theory, individuals must integrate their past experiences, present abilities, and future goals into a coherent sense of self. When adolescents are supported in exploration and allowed to make choices, they are more likely to develop self-confidence and inner consistency. This results in a sense of direction and personal continuity over time.

However, when adolescents struggle to explore or feel pressured to adopt roles imposed by others, they may experience role confusion. This can manifest as uncertainty, frequent changes in goals, or difficulty committing to decisions. While such confusion can be unsettling, it is often temporary. With time, guidance, and opportunities for reflection, most adolescents move toward greater self-clarity. Identity formation during this stage lays the foundation for emotional stability, purposeful decision-making, and healthy adult relationships.

Case Study: Identity Exploration During Adolescence

Background
Riya, a 16-year-old high school student, was academically capable and socially active but felt uncertain about her future direction. Coming from a family of professionals, she was expected to pursue science and prepare for a medical career. However, Riya found herself increasingly drawn to creative writing, debate, and social issues discussed in school clubs.

Identity Exploration Process
During mid-adolescence, Riya began questioning her interests, beliefs, and long-term goals. She experimented with different social roles by joining the school literature club, participating in interschool debates, and volunteering with a local NGO. At the same time, she experienced internal conflict-while her personal interests leaned toward humanities, she feared disappointing her family and deviating from expectations.

Riya also became more self-reflective, often journaling about her strengths, doubts, and values. Exposure to diverse viewpoints through peers and teachers encouraged her to critically evaluate inherited beliefs rather than accept them unquestioningly. This period involved emotional fluctuations, confusion, and anxiety, especially when comparing herself to peers who appeared more certain about their career paths.

Resolution and Outcome

With guidance from a school counsellor and supportive discussions at home, Riya was encouraged to explore her interests without immediate pressure to commit. Over time, she developed a clearer sense of identity that integrated both her creative strengths and her desire to contribute socially. She chose an interdisciplinary academic path combining humanities and social sciences, aligning more closely with her values and abilities.

Psychological Significance

This case reflects what **Erik Erikson** described as the stage of *identity versus role confusion*. Riya's initial uncertainty represented a normal phase of identity exploration. Through experimentation, reflection, and social support, she achieved greater self-clarity and confidence. The case highlights that identity formation is not about immediate certainty, but about navigating exploration in a supportive environment, which ultimately fosters emotional stability and purposeful decision-making.

5.3 Emotional Volatility and Sensitivity

Emotional intensity is a defining feature of adolescence. Hormonal changes, social pressures, and brain development contribute to heightened emotional reactions and mood fluctuations. Adolescents are especially sensitive to peer acceptance, criticism, and social evaluation.

Emotional volatility is one of the most visible and challenging aspects of adolescence. During this stage, young people often experience emotions more intensely and rapidly than in childhood or adulthood. Feelings such as excitement, anger, sadness, embarrassment, or joy can arise suddenly and feel overwhelming. These emotional fluctuations are not simply a matter of immaturity; they are intricately linked to biological, psychological, and social changes occurring during adolescence.

A major contributor to heightened emotional intensity is hormonal change associated with puberty. Fluctuations in hormones influence mood regulation and stress responses, making adolescents more reactive to everyday situations. At the same time, brain development plays a crucial role. Emotional centres of the brain develop earlier than areas responsible for impulse control and emotional regulation, which can result in strong feelings that are difficult to manage effectively. As a result, adolescents may react impulsively or struggle to calm themselves after emotional events.

Social factors further intensify emotional sensitivity. Adolescents place increasing importance on peer relationships, social belonging, and acceptance. Feedback from friends, teachers, and online interactions can strongly affect self-esteem. Criticism, rejection, or embarrassment may feel deeply personal, while approval and validation can significantly boost mood and confidence. This sensitivity to social evaluation explains why adolescents may appear highly self-conscious or emotionally reactive in social settings.

Learning to manage strong emotions during adolescence is a critical developmental task. Through experience, guidance from adults, and supportive relationships, adolescents gradually develop coping skills such as emotional awareness, self-regulation, and perspective-taking. When successfully developed, these skills contribute to psychological resilience, healthier relationships, and emotional stability in adulthood. Although emotional volatility can be challenging, it also reflects the growing emotional depth that supports empathy, passion, and meaningful social connections later in life.

5.4 Risk-Taking, Autonomy, and Decision-Making

Adolescents often experiment with behaviours that involve risk, driven by a desire for independence and novelty. While such behaviour can promote learning and autonomy, it may also expose adolescents to harm.

Risk-taking is a common and developmentally significant feature of adolescence. As young people strive for independence, they increasingly seek new experiences that allow them to assert autonomy and test personal limits. This may include experimenting with new social roles, challenging authority, or engaging in adventurous activities. Such behaviours are often motivated by curiosity, the desire for novelty, and a growing need to make independent choices rather than relying on adult direction.

From a developmental perspective, moderate risk-taking can play a positive role. It helps adolescents learn from real-life experiences, build confidence, and develop critical thinking skills. Trying unfamiliar activities, expressing independent opinions, or taking responsibility for decisions contributes to self-growth and prepares adolescents for adult roles. However, the same drive for exploration can sometimes lead to poor judgment, especially when decisions are made impulsively or under peer pressure.

Biological and cognitive factors also influence adolescent decision-making. While adolescents are capable of logical reasoning, impulse control and long-term planning are still maturing. As a result, short-term rewards may be prioritized over potential long-term consequences. Social influence further heightens risk, as adolescents may engage in behaviours they would otherwise avoid in order to gain peer acceptance or avoid rejection.

Developing sound judgment during adolescence requires a balance between freedom and support. Clear guidance, consistent boundaries, and open communication from parents, educators, and mentors help adolescents evaluate risks more thoughtfully. Providing opportunities for **safe decision-making**, such as supervised independence and structured responsibilities, allows adolescents to practice autonomy without excessive harm. When supported effectively, adolescents learn responsibility, self-control, and decision-making skills that form the foundation for healthy, independent adulthood.

Multiple Choice Questions (MCQs)

1. Which cognitive ability typically develops strongly during adolescence?

A. Reflexive thinking

B. Concrete sensory perception

C. Abstract and hypothetical reasoning

D. Trial-and-error learning

Answer: C. Abstract and hypothetical reasoning

2. According to Erik Erikson, the primary psychosocial challenge of adolescence is:

A. Trust vs. mistrust

B. Autonomy vs. shame

C. Initiative vs. guilt

D. Identity vs. role confusion

Answer: D. Identity vs. role confusion

3. Why are adolescents particularly sensitive to peer approval and criticism?

A. Peer relationships replace all family influence

B. Emotional brain regions develop earlier than regulatory control

C. Adolescents lack logical thinking skills

D. Social interaction is biologically reduced

Answer: B. Emotional brain regions develop earlier than regulatory control

4. Which factor most strongly contributes to emotional volatility during adolescence?

A. Decline in cognitive abilities

B. Complete brain maturation

C. Hormonal changes and ongoing brain development

D. Reduced social interaction

Answer: C. Hormonal changes and ongoing brain development

5. Which approach best supports healthy decision-making and autonomy in adolescents?

A. Strict control with no independence

B. Complete freedom without guidance

C. Supportive boundaries with safe decision-making opportunities

D. Punishment-focused discipline

Answer: C. Supportive boundaries with safe decision-making opportunities

Short Answer Questions

1. What is meant by abstract thinking in adolescence?
2. Why is identity exploration considered a central task of adolescence?

3. How do hormonal changes influence emotional reactions during adolescence?
4. What is emotional volatility, and why is it common in adolescents?
5. How does peer acceptance affect adolescent self-esteem?
6. Why is guided autonomy important in adolescent decision-making?

Long Answer Questions

1. Explain the development of abstract and hypothetical thinking during adolescence and its impact on learning and self-reflection.
2. Discuss identity formation in adolescence with reference to Erik Erikson's concept of identity versus role confusion.
3. Analyse the causes and consequences of emotional sensitivity and mood fluctuations during adolescence.
4. Examine the role of peer influence in shaping adolescent behaviour, emotions, and decision-making.
5. Evaluate the positive and negative aspects of risk-taking behaviour in adolescence.

6

Early Adulthood – Intimacy, Responsibility, and Cognitive Maturity

6.1 Consolidation of Cognitive Abilities

In early adulthood, cognitive functioning becomes more efficient and integrated. Individuals apply accumulated knowledge to real-world problems, balancing logic with experience. Decision-making improves as adults learn to weigh long-term consequences, emotional factors, and practical constraints.

Early adulthood represents a stage in which cognitive abilities reach a high level of organization and effectiveness. Rather than focusing on acquiring basic skills, individuals begin to integrate what they have learned over years of education and life experience. Thinking becomes faster, more flexible, and better coordinated, allowing adults to handle complex tasks with greater confidence. Memory, attention, and reasoning work together smoothly, supporting efficient learning and problem-solving in everyday situations.

At this stage, people rely not only on abstract logic but also on practical understanding gained from real-life experiences. Adults learn to recognize patterns, anticipate outcomes, and adapt strategies based on context. This integration helps them move beyond rigid rules and apply knowledge in nuanced ways, such as resolving workplace challenges, managing relationships, or planning long-term goals.

Decision-making also becomes more balanced and mature. Early adults are better able to consider long-term consequences rather than focusing solely on immediate outcomes. Emotional awareness plays an important role, as individuals learn to factor in feelings, values, and social responsibilities alongside rational analysis. This leads to more thoughtful choices that align with personal priorities and realistic constraints.

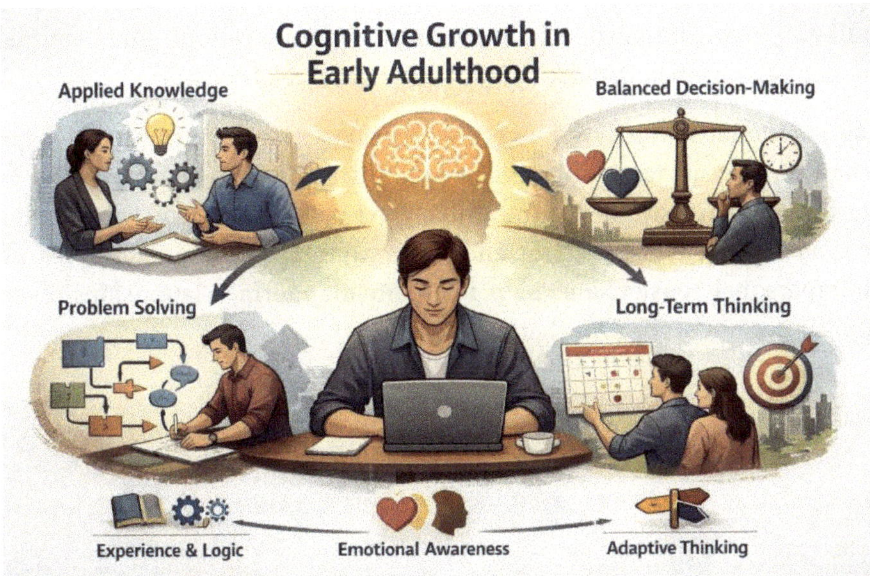

Overall, the consolidation of cognitive abilities in early adulthood supports adaptability and independence. Individuals become capable of adjusting their thinking to changing demands, whether in personal life or professional settings. This cognitive maturity lays a strong foundation for responsible decision-making, problem-solving, and continuous growth throughout adulthood.

6.2 Emotional Intelligence and Relationship Building

Early adulthood is characterized by deepening emotional intelligence and people skills. Adults become better at understanding others' emotions, managing conflicts, and sustaining meaningful relationships. Intimacy, trust, and commitment gain importance, shaping partnerships and friendships.

Early adulthood is a period in which emotional intelligence becomes more refined and actively shapes social interactions. Individuals develop a clearer awareness of their own emotions and learn to recognize emotional cues in others. This heightened sensitivity allows adults to respond with empathy rather than impulsivity, improving communication and mutual understanding in both personal and professional relationships.

As emotional maturity grows, adults become more skilled at managing conflicts and navigating disagreements. Instead of avoiding problems or reacting defensively, they are more likely to engage in constructive dialogue, consider different perspectives, and seek compromise. These abilities reduce interpersonal tension and help maintain long-term relationships, even during periods of stress or change.

Relationships in early adulthood also deepen in quality. Intimacy, trust, and commitment gain greater significance as individuals form close friendships, romantic partnerships, and collaborative work relationships. Emotional intelligence enables adults to balance independence with connection, respect boundaries, and invest in relationships that offer emotional support and shared meaning.

Overall, emotional competence during early adulthood contributes to psychological stability and life satisfaction. The ability to regulate emotions, build trust, and maintain healthy relationships strengthens resilience and well-being. These skills not only enhance social bonds but also provide a supportive foundation for coping with future life challenges.

Adult Role / Responsibility	Key Demands Involved	Skills Required	Possible Outcomes
Employment and Career	Meeting job expectations, skill development, work pressure	Time management, problem-solving, adaptability	Career growth, financial stability, work-related stress
Financial Independence	Budgeting, saving, managing expenses, planning for future	Financial literacy, self-control, planning skills	Economic security or financial anxiety
Partnership and Relationships	Emotional commitment, communication, shared decision-making	Emotional intelligence, conflict resolution	Relationship stability or interpersonal strain
Independent Living	Household management,	Organizational skills, responsibility	Increased autonomy or

	self-care, daily organization		adjustment difficulties
Family Responsibilities	Supporting family members, balancing personal and family needs	Emotional resilience, prioritization	Sense of purpose or role overload

6.3 Transition into Adult Roles and Responsibilities

This stage involves assuming adult roles such as employment, partnership, and independent living. Managing responsibilities related to career, finances, and family demands emotional resilience and organizational skills.

Early adulthood marks a significant shift as individuals move from dependence to greater independence by taking on adult roles and responsibilities. Entering full-time employment, forming long-term partnerships, and managing independent living arrangements require individuals to apply both cognitive and emotional skills developed earlier in life. These new roles bring structure and expectations that shape daily routines and long-term planning.

Managing career demands often becomes a central focus during this stage. Adults must balance professional growth with financial responsibilities such as budgeting, saving, and meeting personal expenses. For many, this period also involves contributing to family responsibilities or preparing for future caregiving roles. Successfully handling these obligations depends on emotional resilience, time management, and the ability to prioritize competing demands.

Adaptation to adult roles plays a crucial role in identity development. When individuals meet responsibilities effectively, they experience increased self-confidence, independence, and a sense of purpose. Achievements in work and personal life reinforce feelings of competence and belonging in society.

These successes help individuals see themselves as capable adults with control over their life direction.

However, difficulty adjusting to adult responsibilities can lead to stress, self-doubt, and identity strain. Unrealistic expectations, financial pressure, or lack of social support may overwhelm individuals during this transition. Supportive environments, guidance, and gradual role adjustment can ease this process, enabling early adults to develop stability and resilience as they move forward in adulthood.

6.4 Coping, Stress Management, and Personal Growth

Early adulthood presents unique stressors, including career uncertainty and relationship challenges. Effective coping strategies-such as problem-solving, emotional regulation, and social support-become essential. Individuals who develop healthy coping mechanisms are better equipped for long-term psychological well-being and continued personal growth.

Early adulthood is often accompanied by multiple sources of stress as individuals navigate new responsibilities, expectations, and uncertainties. Career instability, academic-to-work transitions, financial pressure, and evolving personal relationships can create emotional strain. These challenges require adults to actively manage stress rather than rely on external guidance, making coping skills especially important at this stage.

Effective coping strategies in early adulthood tend to be more deliberate and adaptive. Critical thinking skills help individuals identify stressors, evaluate options, and take constructive action instead of avoiding difficulties. Emotional regulation enables adults to manage anxiety, frustration, or disappointment without becoming overwhelmed. At the same time, seeking social support from friends, family, or mentors provides emotional reassurance and practical advice, reducing feelings of isolation.

Stress management during this period also contributes to personal growth. When individuals learn from setbacks and view challenges as opportunities for development, they strengthen resilience and self-awareness. Healthy habits such as maintaining routines, setting realistic goals, and reflecting on experiences further support emotional balance and confidence.

The ability to cope effectively with stress in early adulthood lays the foundation for long-term psychological well-being. Individuals who develop healthy coping mechanisms are better prepared to handle future life transitions, maintain mental health, and continue growing personally and professionally throughout adulthood.

Multiple Choice Questions (MCQs)

1. Which cognitive change is most characteristic of early adulthood?

A. Decline in memory and attention

B. Dependence on trial-and-error thinking

C. Integration of logic with life experience

D. Predominantly egocentric reasoning

Answer: C. Integration of logic with life experience

2. Emotional intelligence in early adulthood primarily helps individuals to:

A. Avoid emotional situations

B. Suppress all emotional responses

C. Understand and manage emotions in self and others

D. Eliminate interpersonal conflicts completely

Answer: C. Understand and manage emotions in self and others

3. Which of the following is a key feature of relationships in early adulthood?

A. Temporary and experimental bonds

B. Reduced need for trust

C. Emphasis on intimacy, commitment, and trust

D. Complete emotional independence

Answer: C. Emphasis on intimacy, commitment, and trust

4. Successfully adapting to adult roles such as career and independent living most often leads to:

A. Identity confusion

B. Increased self-confidence and sense of purpose

C. Emotional detachment

D. Dependence on external guidance

Answer: B. Increased self-confidence and sense of purpose

5. Which coping strategy is most associated with long-term psychological well-being in early adulthood?

A. Avoidance of stressful situations

B. Emotional suppression

C. Problem-solving and social support

D. Constant comparison with peers

Answer: C. Problem-solving and social support

Short Answer Questions

1. What is meant by the consolidation of cognitive abilities in early adulthood?

2. How does emotional intelligence influence relationship building during early adulthood?
3. Why is intimacy considered a central developmental task in early adulthood?
4. Mention any two adult roles commonly assumed during early adulthood.
5. How does effective stress management support personal growth in early adulthood?
6. What challenges may arise if an individual struggles to adapt to adult responsibilities?

Long Answer Questions

1. Explain how cognitive maturity in early adulthood improves decision-making and problem-solving in real-life situations.
2. Discuss the role of emotional intelligence in forming and sustaining intimate relationships during early adulthood.
3. Analyse the psychological impact of transitioning into adult roles such as employment, financial independence, and family responsibilities.
4. Examine the sources of stress commonly faced in early adulthood and evaluate effective coping strategies.
5. "Successful adaptation to adult roles strengthens identity and purpose." Discuss this statement with suitable examples.

7

Middle Adulthood – Emotional Balance and Life Reassessment

7.1 Psychological Stability and Emotional Regulation

Middle adulthood is often associated with increased emotional stability and self-regulation. Individuals typically gain better control over emotional reactions, responding more thoughtfully rather than impulsively.

Middle adulthood is commonly marked by a noticeable strengthening of emotional balance and psychological steadiness. Compared to earlier life stages, individuals at this phase tend to respond to situations with greater composure and deliberation. Emotional reactions become less intense and less impulsive, as adults develop a deeper awareness of their feelings and the ability to manage them effectively. This improved regulation is largely shaped by accumulated life experiences, which help individuals understand that most challenges are temporary and manageable.

With maturity, adults become better at recognizing emotional triggers and choosing appropriate responses. Instead of reacting immediately to frustration, disappointment, or stress, they are more likely to pause, reflect, and evaluate the situation objectively. This reflective capacity allows them to regulate anger, anxiety, or sadness in constructive ways, such as through communication, planning, or seeking support. As a result, emotional volatility tends to decrease, contributing to greater psychological stability.

Life experience also plays a key role in perspective-taking during middle adulthood. Having faced and resolved various personal, professional, and social challenges over time, individuals are better equipped to assess the relative importance of stressful events. Setbacks are less likely to be perceived as overwhelming or catastrophic. This perspective reduces emotional reactivity and promotes resilience, enabling adults to remain focused and adaptive even under pressure.

For example, a mid-career professional confronted with workplace restructuring may initially feel uncertainty or concern. However, rather than reacting with panic or withdrawal, they are more likely to draw on prior experiences, assess available options, and engage in problem-solving. Emotional restraint, combined with practical decision-making, allows them to cope more effectively. Overall, the enhanced emotional regulation characteristic of middle adulthood supports stable mental health, stronger relationships, and sustained personal well-being.

7.2 Generativity and Contribution to Society

A central psychological concern in middle adulthood is contributing meaningfully to the next generation through parenting, mentoring, teaching, or community involvement. This reflects the idea of generativity emphasized by Erik Erikson, where adults seek purpose beyond personal achievement.

A defining psychological theme of middle adulthood is the desire to contribute meaningfully to others and to society at large. At this stage, individuals often shift their focus from self-centred goals toward activities that nurture, guide, or support the next generation. This outward orientation reflects the concept of **generativity**, a stage highlighted in psychosocial theory by **Erik Erikson**, in which adults seek a sense of purpose through lasting contributions rather than solely through personal success.

Generativity is expressed in many forms, including parenting, mentoring, teaching, leadership, and community service. Adults in middle adulthood often feel motivated to pass on knowledge, skills, values, and life lessons accumulated through experience. This process benefits both the individual and society: while younger people gain guidance and support, the adult experiences a renewed sense of meaning, relevance, and continuity. Engaging in generative roles helps individuals feel that their lives have impact beyond immediate personal outcomes.

Psychologically, generativity supports emotional well-being and identity stability. When adults perceive that they are useful and making a positive difference, they are more likely to experience satisfaction and reduced feelings of stagnation or emptiness. In contrast, a lack of opportunities to contribute may lead to self-doubt or a sense that one's efforts no longer matter. Thus, generativity plays a protective role in mental health during middle adulthood.

For instance, an experienced teacher who mentors younger colleagues may find deep fulfilment in shaping future professionals. By sharing classroom strategies, offering emotional support, and modelling professional ethics, the teacher reinforces their own sense of competence and social value. This contribution strengthens personal purpose while also enhancing the quality of education for future generations. Overall, generativity in middle adulthood reflects a mature psychological orientation-one that emphasizes responsibility, legacy, and meaningful connection with society.

7.3 Midlife Evaluation and Identity Reassessment

Middle adulthood often involves reassessing life goals, achievements, and unmet aspirations. Rather than a dramatic "midlife crisis," many individuals experience a reflective phase that leads to recalibration of priorities. This reassessment can foster psychological growth if approached constructively.

Middle adulthood frequently brings a period of reflection in which individuals reassess their life direction, accomplishments, and unrealized goals. This phase is not necessarily marked by emotional turmoil or crisis; rather, it often involves thoughtful self-examination shaped by accumulated life experience. Adults begin to compare earlier aspirations with current realities, prompting questions about meaning, fulfilment, and long-term priorities.

Unlike the popular notion of a sudden "midlife crisis," many people experience this stage as a gradual and constructive evaluation of identity. Individuals may reflect on career satisfaction, relationships, health, and personal values. Through this process, they often recognize that success and happiness are not fixed concepts but evolving ones. This realization allows adults to adjustxpectations and redefine what constitutes a meaningful life at this stage.

Identity reassessment during middle adulthood can serve as a catalyst for psychological growth. By acknowledging both achievements and limitations, individuals gain a more realistic and compassionate understanding of themselves. This self-awareness supports adaptive decision-making, such as setting new goals, letting go of unrealistic pressures, or investing energy in areas that provide deeper satisfaction. When approached with openness rather than regret, reassessment strengthens emotional maturity and self-acceptance.

For example, an individual who chooses to shift focus from aggressive career advancement toward personal well-being or increased family involvement is not displaying decline but healthy adaptation. Such a change reflects alignment between inner values and outward behaviour. By redefining identity in a way that matches current needs and priorities, adults enhance their sense of balance and purpose. Overall, midlife evaluation in middle adulthood is best understood as a process of recalibration-one that can lead to renewed clarity, resilience, and psychological well-being.

7.4 Coping with Change and Role Transitions

This stage includes coping with changing family roles, health awareness, and professional plateaus. Successful adaptation depends on flexibility and emotional resilience. Adults who accept change as part of development maintain higher psychological well-being.

Middle adulthood is characterized by multiple transitions that require individuals to adapt to changing roles and expectations. Shifts in family dynamics, increased awareness of health and aging, and changes in professional trajectories-such as career plateaus or leadership transitions-can challenge an individual's sense of stability. These changes often arrive simultaneously, making this life stage psychologically demanding yet rich with opportunities for growth.

Effective coping during this period depends largely on flexibility and emotional resilience. Adults who view change as a natural part of development are better equipped to adjust without excessive distress. Rather than resisting new realities, they learn to reinterpret transitions as chances to redefine priorities and explore new roles. Emotional resilience enables individuals to tolerate uncertainty, manage loss, and remain engaged with life despite disruptions to familiar routines.

Family role transitions are particularly significant in middle adulthood. Parents may experience emotional strain as children become independent, while adults may also take on caregiving responsibilities for aging parents. Although these shifts can initially evoke feelings of loss, loneliness, or anxiety, many individuals eventually adapt by finding new sources of meaning. Reinvesting time in personal interests, friendships, or partner relationships often helps restore emotional balance.

For example, parents whose children leave home may first struggle with a sense of emptiness or reduced purpose. Over time, however, many rediscover neglected hobbies, strengthen marital or social bonds, and develop a renewed sense of autonomy. This adjustment reflects healthy coping rather than psychological decline. Overall, adults who accept role transitions with openness and adaptability tend to maintain higher levels of psychological well-being, demonstrating that coping with change in middle adulthood can foster resilience, self-renewal, and sustained emotional health.

Multiple Choice Questions (MCQs)

1. Which psychological characteristic is most commonly associated with middle adulthood?

A. Increased impulsivity   B. Emotional instability

C. Greater emotional regulation   D. Heightened dependency

Answer: C. Greater emotional regulation

2. The concept of *generativity* in middle adulthood primarily refers to:

A. Achieving financial independence

B. Focusing on personal pleasure

C. Contributing to the well-being of the next generation

D. Revisiting unresolved childhood conflicts

Answer: C. Contributing to the well-being of the next generation

3. Midlife evaluation is best described as:

A. A sudden psychological breakdown

B. A period of denial about aging

C. A reflective reassessment of goals and priorities

D. A complete rejection of past achievements

Answer: C. A reflective reassessment of goals and priorities

4. Which factor most strongly supports successful coping with role transitions in middle adulthood?

A. Avoidance of change

B. Emotional rigidity

C. Flexibility and resilience

D. Dependence on others for decision-making

Answer: C. Flexibility and resilience

5. Parents adjusting to children leaving home often demonstrate healthy adaptation when they:

A. Withdraw from social relationships

B. Experience long-term emotional decline

C. Rediscover personal interests and relational balance

D. Completely disengage from family roles

Answer: C. Rediscover personal interests and relational balance

Short Answer Questions

1. What is meant by emotional regulation in middle adulthood?
2. Define generativity and explain its importance during middle adulthood.
3. How does life experience contribute to psychological stability in middle adulthood?
4. What is midlife evaluation, and why is it considered a normal developmental process?
5. Mention two common role transitions experienced during middle adulthood.
6. How does flexibility help adults cope with change during middle adulthood?

Long Answer Questions

1. Explain the concept of emotional balance in middle adulthood and discuss how it influences decision-making and relationships.
2. Analyse the role of generativity in promoting psychological well-being and social responsibility during middle adulthood.

3. Discuss midlife evaluation and identity reassessment, highlighting how this process can lead to personal growth rather than crisis.

4. Examine the psychological challenges associated with changing family and professional roles in middle adulthood.

5. Describe how emotional resilience supports successful adaptation to life changes during middle adulthood, using relevant examples.

8

Late Adulthood – Wisdom, Memory, and Emotional Resilience

8.1 Cognitive Changes and Adaptive Thinking

Late adulthood involves gradual changes in cognitive speed and memory, though not all abilities decline equally. While processing speed may slow, accumulated knowledge and life experience often remain strong. Older adults compensate for cognitive changes through strategies such as routines and external memory aids.

Late adulthood is characterized by noticeable yet highly variable changes in cognitive functioning. One of the most common shifts is a gradual reduction in processing speed, meaning that older adults may take longer to absorb information or respond to complex stimuli. Short-term memory, particularly the ability to quickly recall recent details such as names or appointments, may also become less efficient. However, these changes do not imply a uniform or global decline in intelligence.

Importantly, many cognitive abilities remain stable or even strengthen with age. Knowledge accumulated over a lifetime-often referred to as crystallized intelligence-continues to be a major asset in late adulthood. Skills related to reasoning, judgment, problem interpretation, and understanding complex social situations are often preserved because they rely on experience rather than speed. Older adults frequently draw upon past learning and life lessons to approach problems more thoughtfully and holistically.

Adaptive thinking plays a crucial role in maintaining cognitive effectiveness during this stage of life. Rather than relying solely on rapid recall, older individuals often develop compensatory strategies to support everyday functioning. These may include establishing structured routines, using written notes or digital reminders, organizing tasks systematically, and prioritizing activities that match their strengths. Such strategies reduce cognitive load and help maintain independence and confidence.

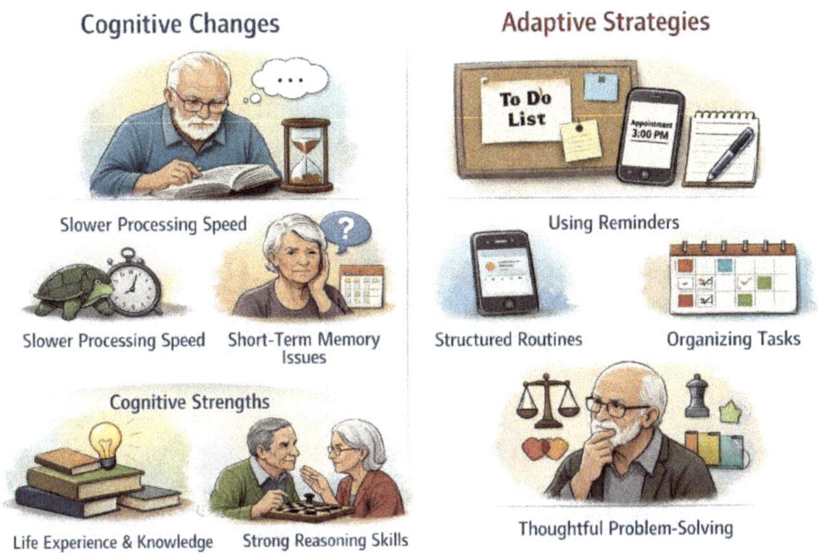

For example, an older adult might struggle to remember new names during social interactions but demonstrate exceptional decision-making in situations requiring careful judgment, ethical reasoning, or long-term planning. This reflects a shift from speed-based cognitive performance to experience-based competence. Overall, cognitive aging in late adulthood is best understood not as simple decline, but as a process of adaptation in which individuals adjust how they think, remember, and solve problems to continue functioning effectively and meaningfully.

8.2 Emotional Well-Being and Positivity Bias

Research suggests that older adults often experience improved emotional regulation and a greater focus on positive experiences. This aligns with socioemotional selectivity theory proposed by Laura Carstensen, which explains why aging individuals prioritize emotionally meaningful relationships.

Late adulthood is often associated with enhanced emotional balance rather than emotional decline. Research in lifespan psychology shows that many older adults become better at managing their emotions, responding more calmly to stress, and recovering more quickly from negative experiences. One notable pattern observed at this stage is the *positivity bias*-a tendency to attend more to pleasant memories, emotions, and experiences while giving less emphasis to negative ones. This shift contributes significantly to emotional well-being and life satisfaction in later years.

EMOTIONAL WELL-BEING AND POSITIVITY BIAS

A Focus on Positive Experiences

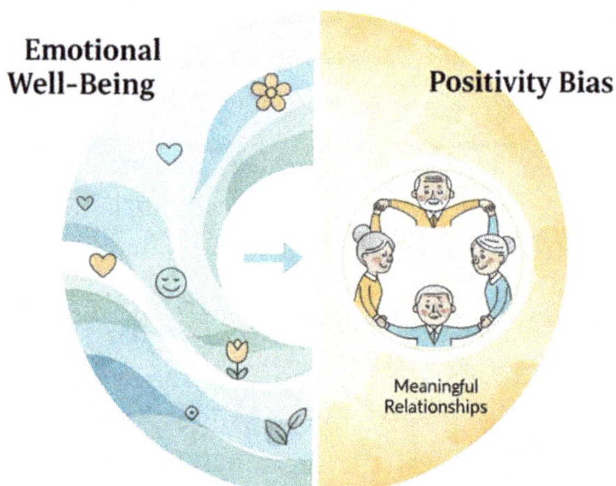

A key explanation for this pattern is **socioemotional selectivity theory** , proposed by Laura Carstensen. According to this theory, as individuals become more aware of the limited nature of time, their motivational priorities change. Rather than focusing on future-oriented goals such as achievement or expansion of social networks, older adults place greater value on emotionally meaningful goals. These include maintaining close relationships, experiencing emotional comfort, and deriving meaning from everyday interactions.

As a result, older adults often become more selective about how they invest their emotional energy. They may consciously avoid conflict, disengage from stressful relationships, and seek environments that promote emotional peace. This selectivity does not reflect social withdrawal or isolation, but rather intentional emotional regulation aimed at maximizing well-being.

For example, many retired individuals choose to narrow their social circles, spending less time on casual or demanding relationships while investing deeply in bonds with close family members or long-term friends. By prioritizing relationships that provide warmth, trust, and mutual understanding, they enhance emotional satisfaction and stability. Overall, emotional aging in late adulthood reflects a shift toward wisdom-based regulation, where emotional depth and positivity become central to psychological health.

8.3 Coping with Loss, Aging, and Role Change

Late adulthood frequently involves coping with bereavement, declining health, and loss of occupational roles. Psychological resilience is shaped by social support, belief systems, and adaptive coping strategies. Acceptance and meaning-making play crucial roles in emotional stability. Late adulthood often brings profound life transitions that require significant psychological adjustment. Common experiences during this stage include the loss of a spouse or peers, increased awareness of physical limitations, and the transition away from long-held occupational roles due to retirement. These changes can challenge an individual's sense of identity, independence, and emotional security. However, the way older adults cope with these experiences varies widely and is strongly influenced by resilience and support systems.

Psychological resilience in late adulthood is shaped by several interrelated factors. Social support from family, friends, and community networks provides emotional comfort and reduces feelings of isolation during periods of loss. Personal belief systems-such as spiritual values, cultural traditions, or philosophical outlooks-often help individuals interpret loss in a broader, more meaningful context. In addition, adaptive coping strategies such as problem-focused coping, emotional acceptance, and positive reframing enable older adults to manage stress more effectively.

Acceptance and meaning-making are particularly important for emotional stability at this stage of life. Rather than resisting inevitable changes, many older adults learn to acknowledge loss as a natural part of the life course. By finding meaning in past achievements, relationships, and ongoing contributions, they preserve a coherent sense of self despite changing roles. This reflective process allows them to integrate loss into their life narrative without being overwhelmed by it.

For instance, an older adult who experiences role loss after retirement may initially struggle with feelings of emptiness or reduced self-worth. However, by engaging in community volunteering, mentoring younger individuals, or participating in social service activities, they can reestablish a sense of purpose and usefulness. Such engagement not only reinforces identity but also fosters emotional well-being by affirming that one's value extends beyond formal employment. Thus, successful coping in late adulthood involves adaptation, acceptance, and the ability to redefine meaning in changing life circumstances.

8.4 Wisdom, Reflection, and Life Meaning

Wisdom in late adulthood reflects the integration of knowledge, emotional insight, and ethical understanding. Reflection on life experiences often leads to acceptance and inner peace. Older adults who find meaning in their life narratives report higher well-being.

Late adulthood is often marked by the emergence of wisdom, a quality that goes beyond intelligence or factual knowledge. Wisdom reflects the integration of life experience, emotional understanding, and moral judgment developed over decades. Through repeated exposure to success, failure, relationships, and loss, older adults gain a broader and more balanced perspective on life. This integration enables them to respond to complex situations with patience, empathy, and thoughtful consideration rather than impulsive reaction.

Reflection plays a central role in the development of wisdom during this stage. Older adults frequently engage in life review, consciously or unconsciously revisiting past experiences to evaluate their choices, relationships, and achievements. This reflective process allows individuals to make sense of both positive and painful events, reducing regret and fostering acceptance. By viewing life as a coherent narrative rather than a series of isolated incidents, many older adults achieve a sense of inner peace and psychological closure.

Finding meaning in one's life story is intricately linked to emotional well-being in late adulthood. Older individuals who are able to recognize purpose in their contributions-such as raising a family, supporting others, or overcoming adversity-tend to report greater life satisfaction. Meaning does not necessarily arise from extraordinary accomplishments but from recognizing the value of everyday acts, relationships, and personal growth across the lifespan.

A clear example of wisdom in action can be seen when grandparents share life lessons with younger generations. Through storytelling, advice, and guidance, they pass on insights shaped by experience, emotional maturity, and ethical reflection. These interactions not only benefit younger individuals but also reinforce the older adult's sense of relevance and fulfilment. Thus, wisdom in late adulthood serves both personal and social functions, enriching emotional well-being while strengthening intergenerational bonds and sustaining a deep sense of life meaning.

Multiple Choice Questions (MCQs)

1. Which cognitive ability is most likely to remain strong in late adulthood despite slower processing speed?

A. Short-term recall

B. Working memory

C. Accumulated knowledge and life experience

D. Reaction time

Answer: C

2. The tendency of older adults to focus more on positive experiences and emotions is known as:

A. Emotional suppression

B. Cognitive rigidity

C. Positivity bias

D. Emotional disengagement

Answer: C

3. According to socioemotional selectivity theory, why do older adults prioritize close relationships?

A. Reduced social skills

B. Increased dependence on others

C. Awareness of limited time and emotional goals

D. Decline in social interest

Answer: C

4. Which strategy best illustrates adaptive coping with age-related cognitive changes?

A. Avoiding complex tasks

B. Relying solely on memory

C. Using routines and external reminders

D. Reducing daily activities entirely

Answer: C

5. Which behaviour most clearly reflects wisdom in late adulthood?

A. Seeking constant novelty

B. Competing with younger adults

C. Reflective storytelling and ethical guidance

D. Avoiding discussion of past experiences

Answer: C

Short Answer Questions

1. What types of cognitive changes are commonly observed in late adulthood?
2. Define positivity bias and explain its role in emotional well-being among older adults.
3. How does socioemotional selectivity influence social relationships in late adulthood?
4. What is meant by adaptive coping in the context of aging?
5. Why is acceptance considered important for emotional resilience in late adulthood?
6. How does reflective life review contribute to wisdom in older adults?

Long Answer Questions

1. Discuss the nature of cognitive aging in late adulthood, highlighting both areas of decline and areas of stability.

2. Explain socioemotional selectivity theory and analyse how it helps explain emotional regulation and relationship choices in older adults.

3. Examine the psychological challenges associated with loss, aging, and role transitions in late adulthood, and discuss strategies that promote resilience.

4. Analyse the concept of wisdom in late adulthood and explain how life reflection contributes to meaning and well-being.

5. Evaluate the role of social support and community engagement in maintaining emotional health among older adults.

6. "Late adulthood is a stage of adaptation rather than decline." Critically discuss this statement with reference to cognitive, emotional, and social changes.

9

Integrating the Lifespan – Continuity, Change, and Psychological Well-Being

9.1 Continuity and Transformation Across Life Stages

Human development reflects both continuity and transformation. While certain personality traits remain stable, emotional responses, cognitive strategies, and social priorities evolve with age. Development is best understood as a layered process where earlier experiences influence later adaptation.

Human development unfolds as a dynamic interplay between stability and change. Rather than being a series of disconnected phases, life stages are interwoven, with earlier experiences shaping how individuals respond to new challenges and opportunities later on. Some core aspects of personality-such as temperament, basic emotional tendencies, or values-often show continuity across the lifespan. These enduring traits provide a sense of identity and coherence as people grow older.

At the same time, development involves significant transformation. Emotional responses mature, cognitive strategies become more refined, and social priorities shift in response to changing roles and environments. For instance, ways of managing stress that are effective in adolescence may be replaced by more reflective or problem-focused approaches in adulthood. Similarly, priorities may move from self-exploration in early life to responsibility, contribution, or legacy in later years. These changes do not erase earlier patterns but build upon them.

Understanding development as a layered process helps explain why individuals adapt differently to similar life events. Early experiences-such as supportive caregiving, emotional security, or exposure to learning opportunities-form a foundation that influences later coping, relationships, and decision-making. However, this foundation is not rigid. New experiences, education, relationships, and personal choices can reshape how earlier traits are expressed over time.

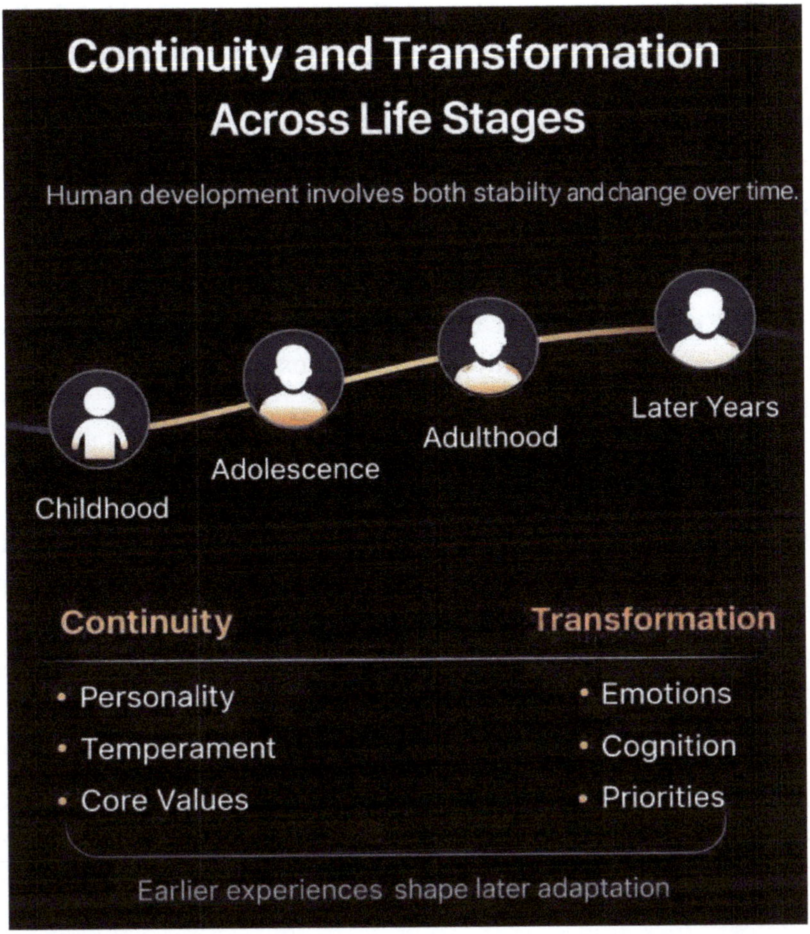

For example, a person who experienced emotional security in childhood may enter adulthood with a stronger capacity for trust and intimacy, supporting healthier relationships. Even as responsibilities evolve-such as managing a career or family-the underlying sense of security continues to guide adaptive behaviour. Thus, human development reflects both continuity in core foundations and transformation in how individuals think, feel, and engage with the world across different stages of life.

9.2 Interdependence of Cognition, Emotion, and Social Context

Psychological growth occurs through the interaction of thinking, feeling, and social environment. Changes in one domain influence others across the lifespan. Supportive environments enhance adaptation, while adverse contexts may hinder emotional well-being.

Psychological development does not occur within isolated compartments of thought, emotion, or social experience. Instead, growth across the lifespan emerges from the continuous interaction among these three domains. How individuals think influences how they feel, emotions shape social behaviour, and social environments, in turn, affect both cognitive functioning and emotional well-being. This interdependence explains why changes in one area often trigger adjustments in others.

Cognition plays a central role in interpreting experiences and regulating emotions. For example, the way a person understands success, failure, or aging affects emotional reactions such as confidence, anxiety, or motivation. Emotional states also influence cognitive processes; stress can impair attention and memory, while positive emotions can enhance creativity and problem-solving. These reciprocal effects highlight that thinking and feeling are deeply connected rather than independent processes.

The social context provides the setting in which cognition and emotion are expressed and shaped. Supportive relationships, meaningful roles, and opportunities for participation promote psychological resilience and adaptability. In contrast, isolation, discrimination, or chronic stress can disrupt emotional balance and negatively affect cognitive performance. Social environments can either buffer individuals from life challenges or intensify vulnerabilities, depending on the quality of support and engagement they offer.

Across the lifespan, this interaction remains vital. For instance, access to lifelong learning programs or intellectually stimulating social activities helps older adults remain mentally active while also fostering a sense of purpose and emotional confidence. Engaging with peers, learning new skills, or contributing to the community reinforces positive emotions and sustains cognitive flexibility. Thus, psychological growth is best understood as an ongoing process shaped by the combined influence of cognition, emotion, and the social world in which individuals live.

9.3 Promoting Mental Well-Being Across the Lifespan

Mental well-being is shaped by adaptive coping, emotional awareness, and social connection at every age. Preventive strategies, education, and community support can strengthen psychological health throughout life. Development does not end with adulthood; growth remains possible at all stages.

Mental well-being is not a static state achieved at a particular age but an ongoing process that evolves throughout life. At every stage, psychological health is influenced by how individuals cope with challenges, understand and manage their emotions, and maintain meaningful social connections. These elements work together to support resilience, life satisfaction, and a sense of purpose across changing life circumstances.

Adaptive coping plays a central role in sustaining mental well-being. As people encounter transitions such as academic pressure, career demands, family responsibilities, health changes, or retirement, the ability to respond flexibly becomes essential. Coping strategies such as problem-solving, emotional regulation, and seeking social support help individuals manage stress more effectively. Over time, people often refine these strategies, learning which responses are most helpful in different situations.

Emotional awareness is equally important across the lifespan. Recognizing emotions, understanding their sources, and expressing them in healthy ways contribute to psychological balance. Emotional skills developed early in life can be strengthened later through reflection, therapy, or self-care practices. Social connection further reinforces well-being by providing belonging, validation, and shared meaning. Supportive relationships with family, friends, or community groups act as protective factors against loneliness and emotional distress.

Preventive approaches, education, and community-based support systems enhance mental health at all ages. Programs that promote stress management, emotional literacy, and social engagement help individuals maintain psychological stability before serious difficulties arise. Importantly, development and growth continue well beyond adulthood. For example, mindfulness practices adopted in later life can improve emotional regulation, reduce stress, and foster acceptance of life changes. This demonstrates that mental well-being can be nurtured and strengthened at every stage, affirming the lifelong potential for psychological growth and adaptation.

9.4 A Holistic View of Growing Minds

Understanding development as a lifelong journey encourages empathy, self-awareness, and social responsibility. Recognizing age-related psychological changes helps individuals and societies support growth, dignity, and well-being across generations.

Viewing human development as a lifelong journey provides a comprehensive understanding of how individuals think, feel, and relate to others across different ages. Rather than limiting growth to childhood or adolescence, a holistic perspective recognizes that psychological change and learning continue throughout life. This approach encourages greater empathy toward people at different life stages and promotes self-awareness by helping individuals understand their own evolving needs, strengths, and limitations.

Recognizing age-related psychological changes is essential for supporting dignity and well-being. Cognitive abilities, emotional regulation, and social roles naturally shift over time, and these changes should be understood as adaptations rather than deficits. When societies acknowledge these transitions, they are better equipped to create supportive environments-such as age-inclusive education, flexible workplaces, and community-based mental health services-that enable individuals to remain engaged and valued at every stage of life.

Dimension	Description	Impact Across the Lifespan	Illustrative Example
Cognitive Development	Continuous change in thinking, learning, and problem-solving abilities	Encourages lifelong learning, adaptability, and intellectual engagement at all ages	Older adults participating in skill-based or educational programs
Emotional Development	Ongoing refinement of emotional awareness, regulation, and empathy	Supports emotional stability, resilience, and mental well-being	Improved emotional understanding through reflection and life experience
Social Development	Evolving social roles, relationships, and responsibilities	Promotes inclusion, belonging, and social cohesion across generations	Community participation and intergenerational interaction
Lifelong Growth Perspective	Development viewed as a continuous journey rather than age-limited stages	Enhances dignity, respect, and support for individuals at every age	Age-inclusive policies and community programs

A holistic view also emphasizes shared social responsibility. Families, institutions, and communities play an active role in shaping developmental outcomes by fostering respect, inclusion, and opportunities for participation across generations. Policies and practices that consider the psychological needs of children, adults, and older persons help reduce marginalization and strengthen social bonds. This perspective moves beyond individual development to highlight collective well-being.

Intergenerational initiatives illustrate the value of this approach. Programs that bring together youth and older adults create spaces for mutual learning, emotional exchange, and perspective-sharing. Younger participants benefit from guidance, experience, and emotional stability, while older individuals gain renewed purpose and social connection. Such interactions enhance emotional understanding and social cohesion, demonstrating that a holistic view of growing minds supports not only individual growth but also healthier, more compassionate societies.

Multiple Choice Questions (MCQs)

1. Which statement best reflects the concept of continuity in lifespan development?

a) Personality completely changes at each life stage

b) Early experiences have no influence on adulthood

c) Certain traits remain stable while adapting over time

d) Development stops after adolescence

Correct Answer: c) Certain traits remain stable while adapting over time

2. Psychological development across the lifespan is best understood as:

a) A sequence of isolated and unrelated stages

b) A process influenced only by biological aging

c) A layered process shaped by earlier experiences and later adaptations

d) A decline in abilities after early adulthood

Correct Answer: c) A layered process shaped by earlier experiences and later adaptations

3. How do cognition, emotion, and social context interact in psychological growth?

a) Each develops independently of the others

b) Social factors influence cognition but not emotion

c) Changes in one domain affect the others

d) Emotional development ends in childhood

Correct Answer: c) Changes in one domain affect the others

4. Which factor most strongly supports mental well-being across all life stages?

a) Avoidance of emotional expression

b) Fixed coping strategies

c) Adaptive coping and social connection

d) Intellectual ability alone

Correct Answer: c) Adaptive coping and social connection

5. What does a holistic view of growing minds emphasize?

a) Psychological growth is limited to early life

b) Aging primarily involves psychological decline

c) Development continues and requires social responsibility across generations

d) Individual growth is unrelated to society

Correct Answer: c) Development continues and requires social responsibility across generations

Short Answer Questions

1. What is meant by continuity in lifespan psychological development?
2. How do early life experiences influence psychological well-being in later stages?
3. Why is the interaction between cognition and emotion important across the lifespan?
4. What role does social context play in maintaining mental well-being at different ages?
5. Define adaptive coping and explain its significance in psychological health.
6. How do intergenerational relationships contribute to holistic development?

Long Answer Questions

1. Discuss how human development reflects both continuity and change across life stages, with suitable examples.

2. Examine the interdependence of cognition, emotion, and social environment in shaping psychological growth throughout life.
3. Explain the importance of promoting mental well-being as a lifelong process rather than a stage-specific goal.
4. Analyse the role of preventive strategies and community support in enhancing psychological well-being across generations.
5. Critically evaluate the concept of a holistic view of growing minds and its relevance for modern societies.
6. Describe how intergenerational programs can promote empathy, emotional understanding, and social cohesion, supporting lifespan development.

References

Chapter 1: Understanding Human Development Across the Lifespan

1. Baltes, P. B. (1987). Theoretical propositions of life-span developmental psychology. *Developmental Psychology*, 23(5), 611–626. https://doi.org/10.1037/0012-1649.23.5.611

2. Lerner, R. M. (2018). *Concepts and theories of human development* (4th ed.). Routledge.

3. Santrock, J. W. (2020). *Life-span development* (17th ed.). McGraw-Hill Education.

Chapter 2: The Infant Mind – Foundations of Perception and Attachment

1. Bowlby, J. (1969). *Attachment and loss: Vol. 1. Attachment*. Basic Books.

2. Ainsworth, M. D. S., Belhar, M. C., Waters, E., & Wall, S. (1978). *Patterns of attachment*. Lawrence Erlbaum.

3. Johnson, M. H. (2011). Interactive specialization: A domain-general framework for human functional brain development. *Developmental Cognitive Neuroscience*, 1(1), 7–21. https://doi.org/10.1016/j.dcn.2010.07.003

Chapter 3: Early Childhood – Language, Imagination, and Emotional Growth

1. Vygotsky, L. S. (1978). *Mind in society*. Harvard University Press.

2. Berk, L. E. (2018). *Development through the lifespan* (7th ed.). Pearson.

3. Ginsburg, K. R. (2007). The importance of play in promoting healthy child development. *Pediatrics*, 119(1), 182–191. https://doi.org/10.1542/peds.2006-2697

Chapter 4: Middle Childhood – Reasoning, Morality, and Social Awareness

1. Piaget, J. (1965). *The moral judgment of the child*. Free Press.
2. Kohlberg, L. (1984). *Essays on moral development, Vol. II*. Harper & Row.
3. Eccles, J. S. (1999). The development of children ages 6–14. *The Future of Children*, 9(2), 30–44.

Chapter 5: Adolescence – Identity Formation and Emotional Intensity

1. Erikson, E. H. (1968). *Identity: Youth and crisis*. W. W. Norton.
2. Steinberg, L. (2014). *Age of opportunity: Lessons from the new science of adolescence*. Houghton Mifflin Harcourt.
3. Casey, B. J., Jones, R. M., & Hare, T. A. (2008). The adolescent brain. *Annals of the New York Academy of Sciences*, 1124, 111–126. https://doi.org/10.1196/annals.1440.010

Chapter 6: Early Adulthood – Intimacy, Responsibility, and Cognitive Maturity

1. Arnett, J. J. (2015). *Emerging adulthood* (2nd ed.). Oxford University Press.
2. Erikson, E. H. (1982). *The life cycle completed*. Norton.
3. Lachman, M. E. (2004). Development in midlife. *Annual Review of Psychology*, 55, 305–331. https://doi.org/10.1146/annurev.psych.55.090902.141521

Chapter 7: Middle Adulthood – Emotional Balance and Life Reassessment

1. McAdams, D. P., & de St. Aubin, E. (1992). A theory of generativity. *Psychological Review*, 100(2), 241–262. https://doi.org/10.1037/0033-295X.100.2.241
2. Levinson, D. J. (1978). *The seasons of a man's life*. Knopf.
3. Ryff, C. D. (1989). Happiness is everything, or is it? *Journal of Personality and Social Psychology*, 57(6), 1069–1081.

Chapter 8: Late Adulthood – Wisdom, Memory, and Emotional Resilience

1. Carstensen, L. L. (2006). The influence of a sense of time on human development. *Science*, 312(5782), 1913–1915. https://doi.org/10.1126/science.1127488
2. Baltes, P. B., & Smith, J. (2008). The fascination of wisdom. *Perspectives on Psychological Science*, 3(1), 56–64.
3. Craik, F. I. M., & Salthouse, T. A. (2011). *The handbook of aging and cognition* (3rd ed.). Psychology Press.

Chapter 9: Integrating the Lifespan – Continuity, Change, and Psychological Well-Being

1. Elder, G. H. (1998). The life course as developmental theory. *Child Development*, 69(1), 1–12.
2. Heckhausen, J., Wrosch, C., & Schulz, R. (2010). A motivational theory of life-span development. *Psychological Review*, 117(1), 32–60. https://doi.org/10.1037/a0017668
3. Diener, E., Oishi, S., & Lucas, R. E. (2015). National accounts of well-being. *American Psychologist*, 70(3), 234–242.

APPENDIX

1. Glossary of Key Terms

Attachment – An emotional bond formed between an infant and caregiver that influences emotional security and later relationships.

Cognitive Development – Age-related changes in thinking, reasoning, memory, and problem-solving abilities.

Emotional Regulation – The ability to manage and respond to emotional experiences in a socially appropriate manner.

Generativity – A psychological concern in adulthood involving contributing to the well-being of future generations.

Identity Formation – The process through which individuals develop a coherent sense of self, values, and life goals.

2. Data Sources and Datasets

Although this book is conceptual and theoretical, it draws upon findings derived from well-established data sources used in developmental psychology research:

- **Longitudinal Human Development Studies**
  (e.g., birth cohort and lifespan tracking studies)
- **National Mental Health Surveys**
  Conducted by governmental and public health agencies
- **Educational and Child Development Surveys**
  Used to assess cognitive, emotional, and social growth across age groups
- **Gerontological and Aging Studies**
  Examining cognitive change, emotional well-being, and aging populations

These data sources collectively inform evidence-based understanding of age-related psychological change.

3. Tools and Frameworks

The following theoretical tools and analytical frameworks underpin the discussions throughout the book:

- **Lifespan Development Framework** – Views development as continuous and multidimensional
- **Psychosocial Development Framework** – Emphasizes emotional and social challenges across life stages
- **Cognitive Development Models** – Explain changes in thinking and reasoning abilities
- **Attachment Framework** – Used to understand emotional bonding and relational security

These frameworks help integrate biological, psychological, and social perspectives on human growth.

4. References for Further Reading

Readers seeking deeper exploration may consult the following authoritative works:

- Baltes, P. B. (1987). *Theoretical propositions of life-span developmental psychology.*
- Berk, L. E. (2018). *Development through the lifespan.*
- Erikson, E. H. (1982). *The life cycle completed.*
- Santrock, J. W. (2020). *Life-span development.*
- Steinberg, L. (2014). *Age of opportunity: Lessons from the new science of adolescence.*

- Carstensen, L. L. (2006). Emotional experience improves with age.
- World Health Organization. (2022). *Mental health and ageing*.

These readings expand theoretical depth and empirical grounding.

5. Future Directions in Lifespan Psychology

Future research and practice in developmental psychology are likely to focus on:

- Neuroscience-informed developmental models
- Mental health promotion across all ages
- Impact of digital technology on cognitive and emotional growth
- Aging populations and successful aging strategies
- Cross-cultural and inclusive developmental frameworks
- Preventive interventions for emotional well-being

Understanding development in rapidly changing social and technological environments remains a key priority.

6. Summary of Key Points

- Psychological development is lifelong and dynamic
- Cognition and emotion evolve in interaction with age, experience, and context
- Each life stage presents distinct psychological tasks and challenges
- Emotional regulation generally strengthens with maturity
- Identity and meaning continue to evolve beyond adolescence
- Aging involves both adaptation and growth , not merely decline

ABOUT THE AUTHORS

Dr. Anu Kant Mital is an eminent psychiatrist, academic, and global mental health consultant with over three decades of experience in clinical psychiatry and psychological sciences. A graduate of Grant

Medical College, Mumbai, he holds an M.D. in Psychiatry, a Ph.D. in Psychology from MAG H University (UK), and an M.A. in Psychology. His extensive training spans clinical hypnotherapy, family therapy (UK), criminology, and biomedical ethics. Dr. Mital has served as a UNESCO Unit Head in Biomedical Ethics (Haifa) and as an External Consultant with the United Nations CISMU. He is currently a Consultant Psychiatrist at several prestigious institutions including Jupiter Hospital, Masina Hospital, and Godbole Heart Hospital. He has held academic leadership roles such as Dean at FIAMC Biomedical Ethics Centre and in the past as the Professor of Psychiatry at R.G. Medical College. His international exposure includes service within the UK NHS and observation at the University of Berne, Switzerland

Kishore Chandrakant Raipurkar is a retired Professor of Mechanical Engineering with over four decades of distinguished experience in higher and technical education under the Government of Maharashtra. He has served in multiple academic leadership roles

including Head of Department, Training and Placement Officer, Controller of Examinations, and In-Charge Principal at reputed government engineering institutions. Holding postgraduate degrees in Mechanical Engineering and Psychology, he uniquely integrates technical expertise with human development, pedagogy, and mentoring. He has designed university curricula, authored academic books, led national-level training programs, and contributed to industry–academia collaboration initiatives. Currently pursuing a Ph.D. in Psychology, he continues to work as a trainer, counselor, and education consultant, with a strong commitment to student employability and social development.

Prof. Dhanashri R. Jadhav is an experienced counselling psychologist with over 5 years of expertise in career and family counselling. She has successfully guided more than 1500 students in career planning,

decision-making, and personal development. As part of her work with CareerNaksha, she has spent 2 years helping students explore educational and professional pathways. At her own initiative, Mind Power Counselling Center, Prof. Jadhav offers therapy for anger and stress management, depression, anxiety, trauma, and personal empowerment. She has conducted 100+ family counselling sessions, focusing on conflict resolution and enhancing family communication. She holds a Master's degree in Psychology from Savitribai Phule Pune University (2015–2017) and is currently pursuing a PhD in Counselling Psychology from Himalayan Garhwal University, Uttarakhand. Her approach blends empathy, insight, and strategic guidance, aimed at empowering individuals to thrive in academic, emotional, and personal spheres.

Dr. Krithika Tharan is a Nutritional Psychologist, TEDx Speaker, and Founder of Hepta Academy and Hepta Senz, integrating psychology, nutrition, and behavioral science to drive holistic wellness. A certified

Zenlp Master Practitioner and corporate trainer, she empowers professionals through evidence-based programs that enhance mental resilience and productivity. Recognised with various awards for social activism and political activism. Krithika has authored acclaimed books on diet and travel and delivered over 300+ media sessions. Her mission is to help organizations cultivate healthier, purpose-driven teams that align wellbeing with peak performance.

10. E-LIBRAIRIE – France (French online bookstore)
11. Everand – India (Everand Book Distributor is based in India)
12. EXLIBRIS – Switzerland
13. Fable – United Kingdom (UK/Europe digital subscription book service)
14. Flipkart – India
15. GANDHI.com – Mexico (Librerías Gandhi)
16. Google Book – United States (Google LLC)
17. Google Audio Book – United States (Google LLC)
18. IBS.IT – Italy Wikipedia
19. Indigo – Canada
20. Kobo – Canada Wikipedia
21. Kindle – United States (Amazon product)
22. LAFELTRINELLI – Italy Wikipedia
23. Lehmanns – Germany
24. Lulu – United States
25. MORAWA – Austria
26. Rakuten Japan – Japan (Rakuten)
27. Smashwords – United States

28. Tolino / Thalia – Germany (Tolino is a German-language eBook ecosystem, Thalia DE)
29. Vivlio – France
30. Saxo – Denmark (Saxo.com)
31. YES24 – South Korea

🎁 You will receive 20 physical author copies FREE to your Indian address.

⭑ You can also receive 5 book reviews:

* 3 reviews by eminent university professors

* 2 reviews from your own group/colleagues/seniors/teachers

www.books.wissira.us

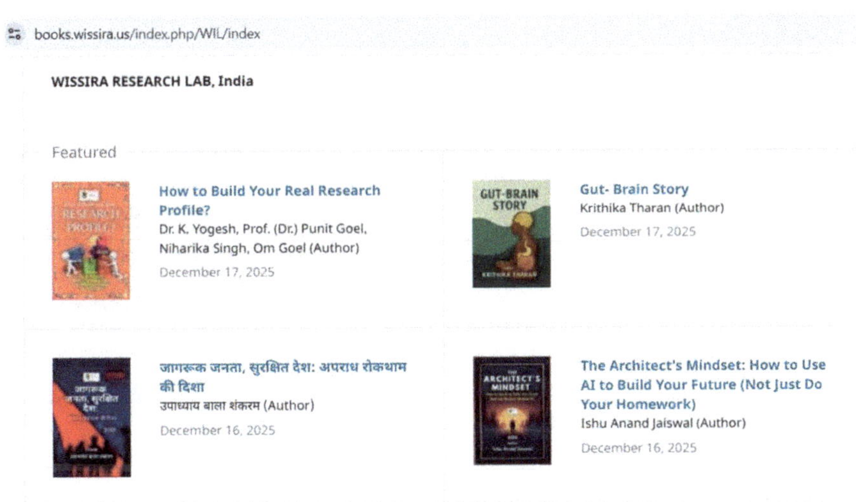

www.books.wissira.us

DOI: https://doi.org/10.63345/book.wrl.2512000324

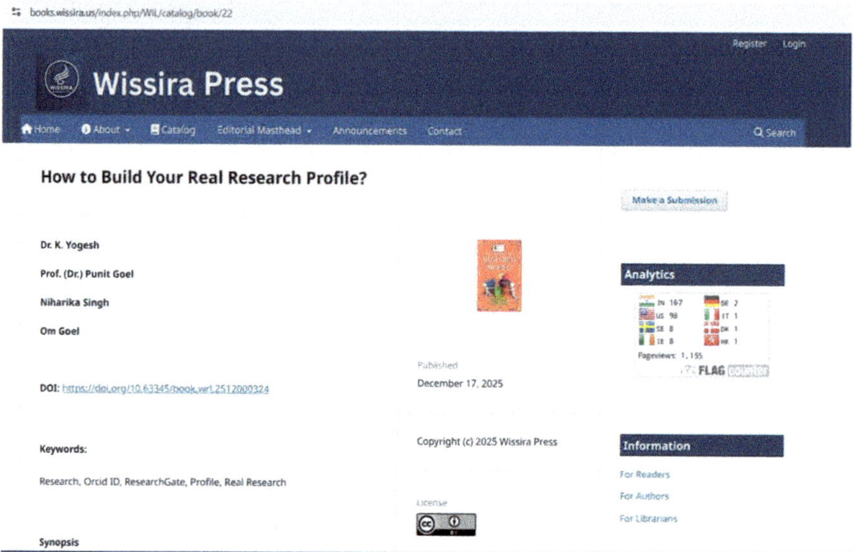

https://books.wissira.us/index.php/WIL/login

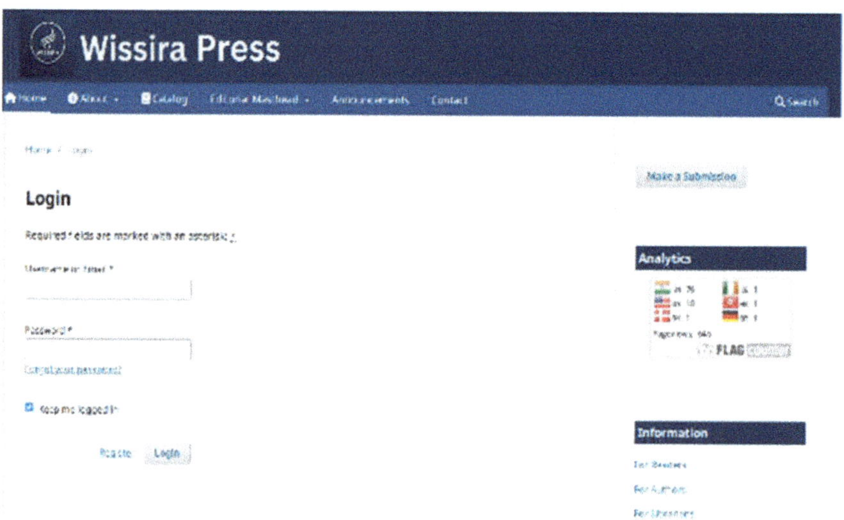

https://books.wissira.us/index.php/WIL/catalog

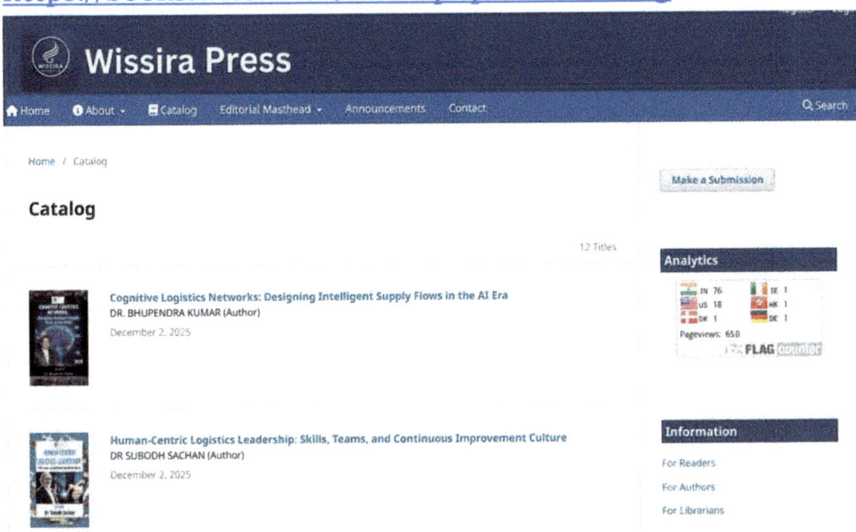

https://books.wissira.us/index.php/WIL/about/contact

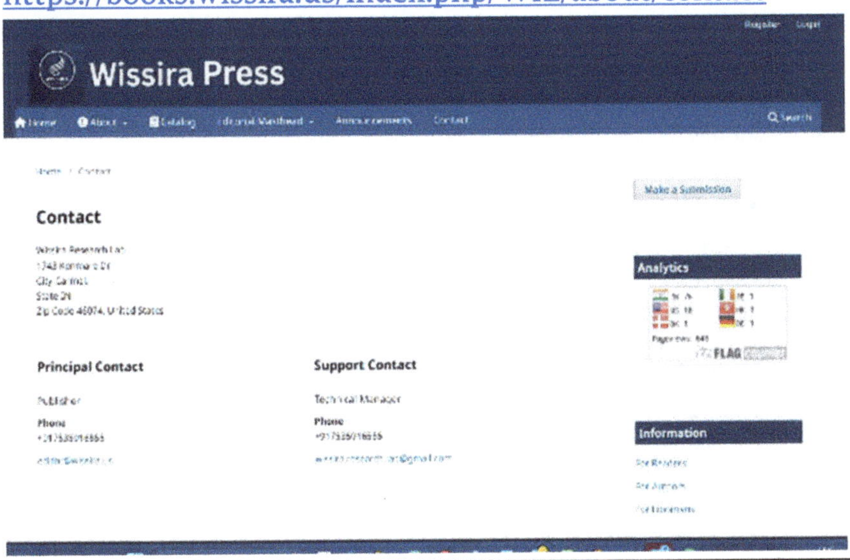

https://www.amazon.in/dp/B0G7MQFD2L

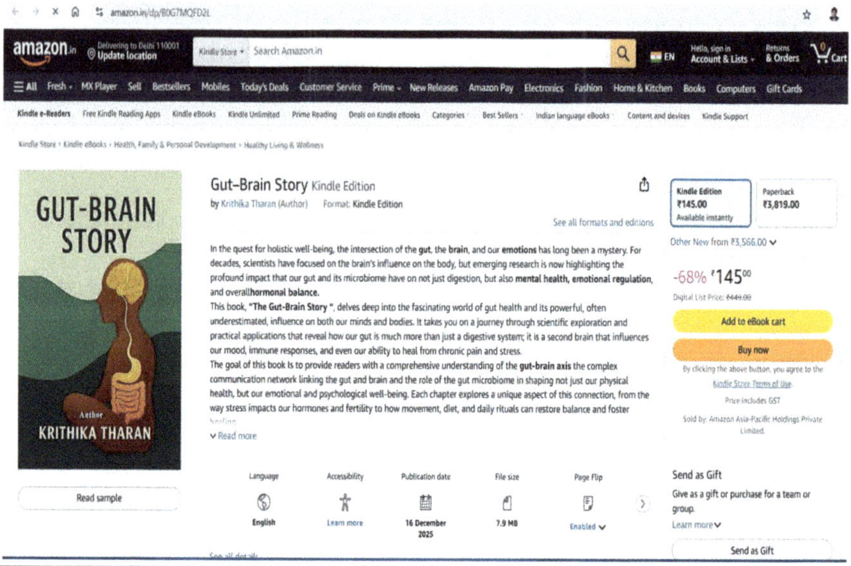

https://books.apple.com/us/book/the-architects-mindset-how-to-use-ai-to-build-your/id6756545876

Flipkart:
https://tinyurl.com/WissieaPressBook250306Human

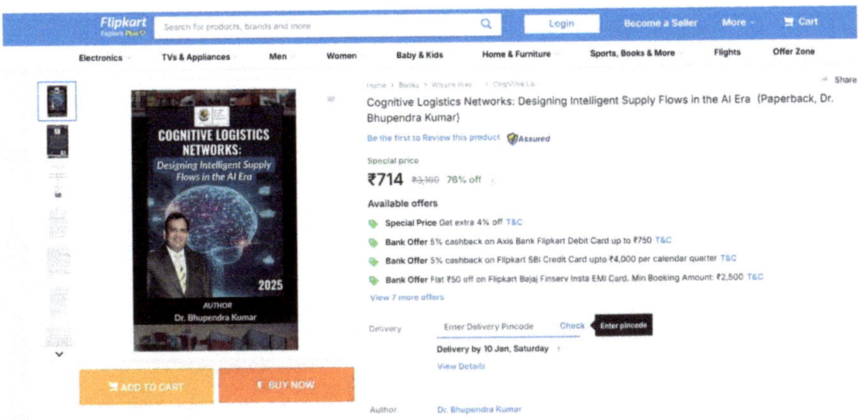

https://shop.vivlio.com/product/9798232547615_9798232547615_10020/human-centric-logistics-leadership-skills-teams-and-continuous-improvement-culture

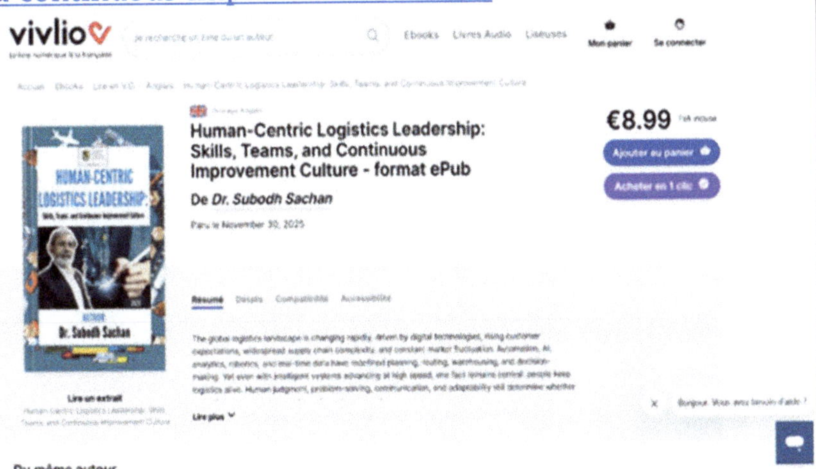

https://fable.co/book/x-9798230804772

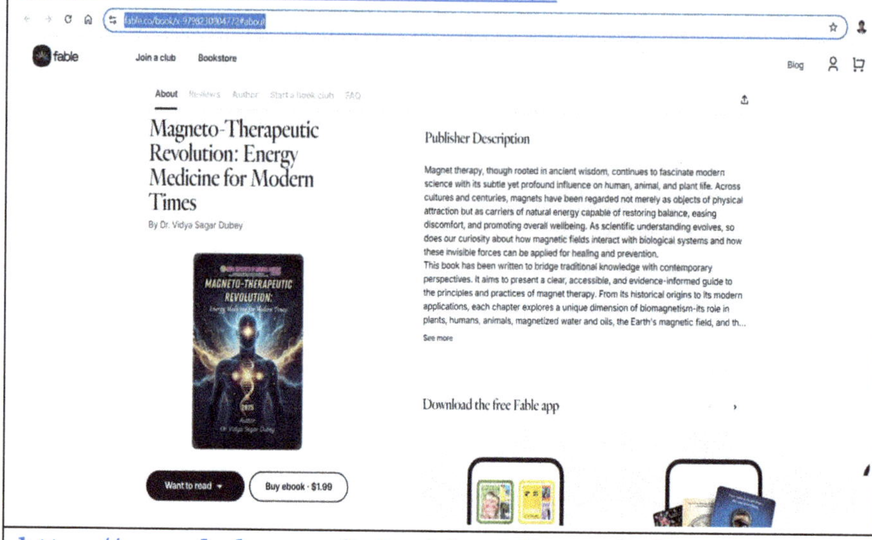

https://www.kobo.com/in/en/ebook/from-shakespeare-to-tagore-reinterpreting-english-literature-through-indian-sensibility?sId=070486d4-8aef-4220-a1d2-26bb2ba8ecb6&ssId=3FJLsnB4eTMdnS31kaTcM

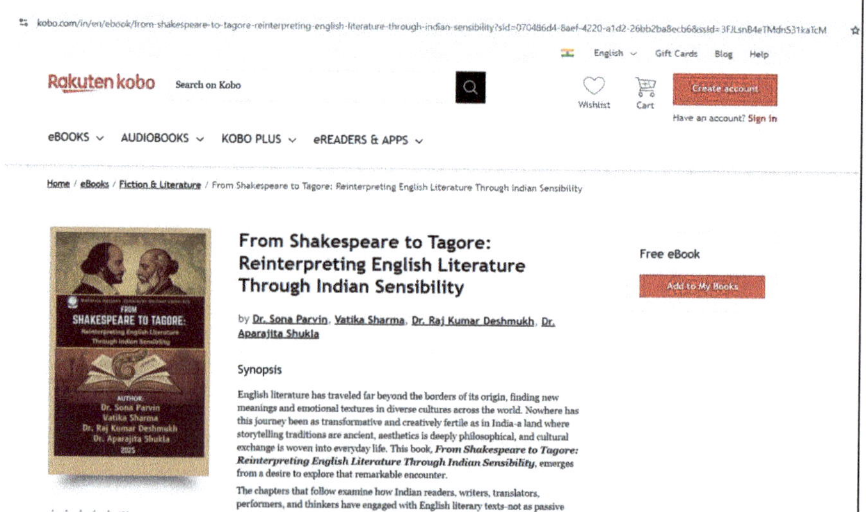

https://www.lulu.com/shop/dr-subodh-sachan/human-centric-logistics-leadership/ebook/product-rmj4erq.html?q=Human-Centric+Logistics+Leadership%3A+Skills%2C+Teams%2C+and+Continuous+Improvement+Culture&page=1&pageSize=

4

https://play.google.com/store/audiobooks/details?id=AQAAAEDqoRHh6M

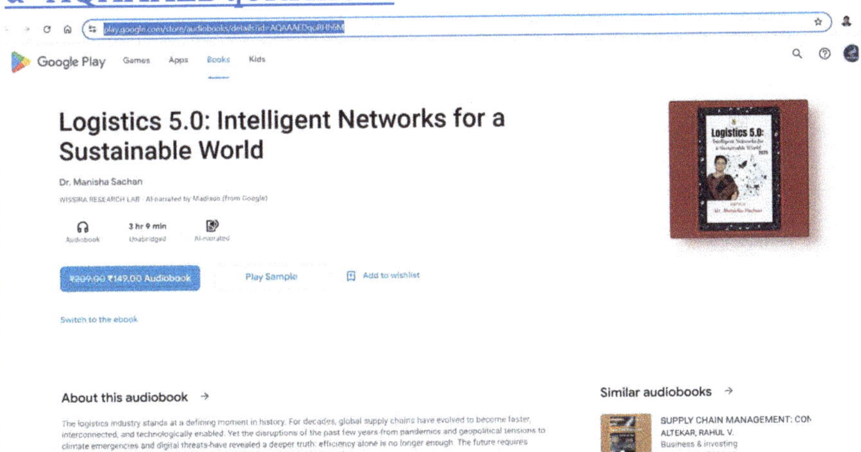

https://play.google.com/store/books/details?id=TbmfEQAAQBAJ

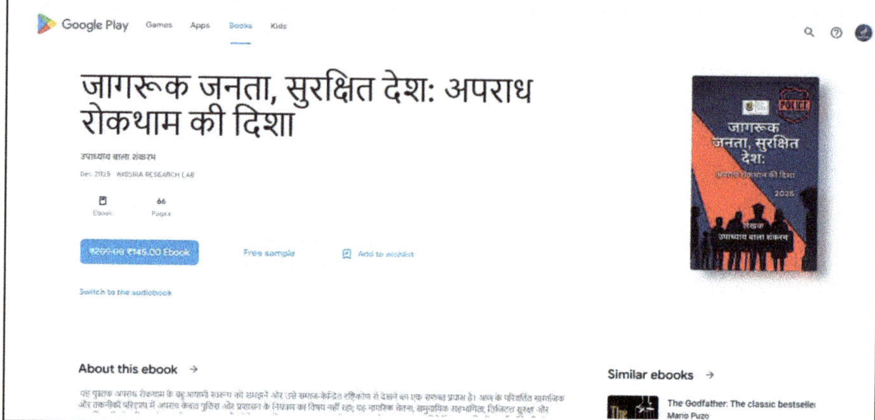

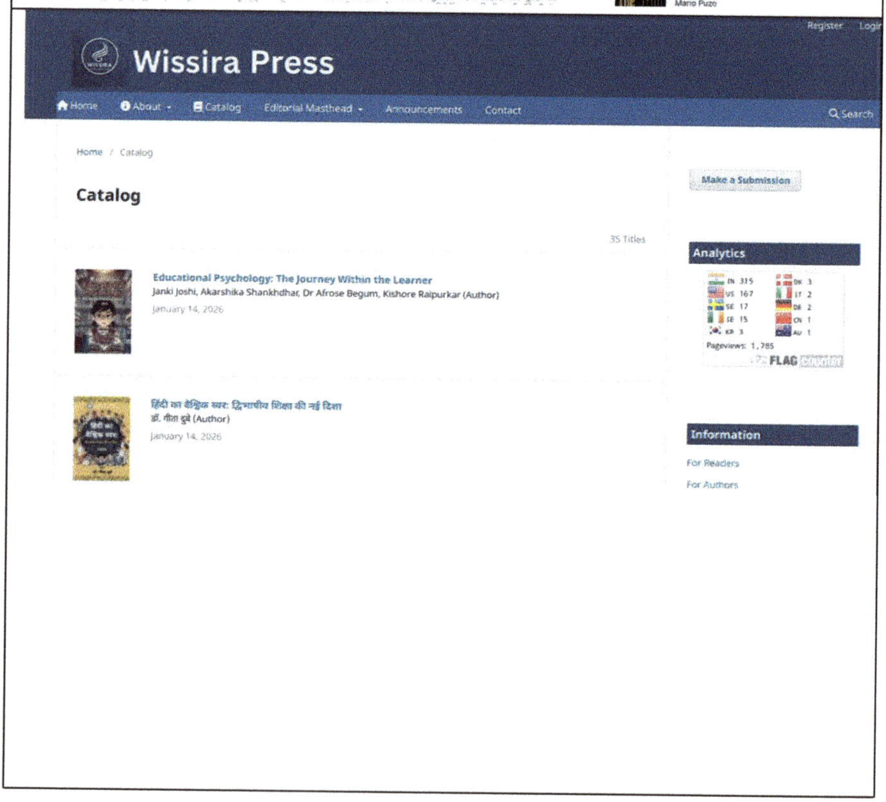

Amazon Kindle

Amazon

Flipkart

LULU

Apple Books

Barnes & Nobles

Everand

Fable

Kobo

Analytics

IN	135	IT	1
US	84	DK	1
SE	8	HK	1
IE	8	DE	1

Pageviews: 1,012

FLAG counter

Information

For Readers

For Authors

For Librarians

Keywords

sustain long-term operational excellence.

Across the nine chapters of this work, readers will find a structured and practical approach to understanding how leadership influences logistics outcomes. Beginning with the foundations of human-centric leadership, the book explores essential competencies such as communication, empathy, decision-making, and ethical responsibility-skills that enable leaders to build credibility and trust in high-pressure environments. It then moves deeper into the dynamics of teamwork, motivation, and empowerment, highlighting how resilient and collaborative teams become the backbone of

Smashwords

Tolino

Vivlio

Google Books

---

www.ingramcontent.com/pod-product-compliance
Ingram Content Group UK Ltd.
Pitfield, Milton Keynes, MK11 3LW, UK
UKHW021411190726
13845UKWH00028B/1016